ADVANCE PRAISE FOR *A DREAM FORECLOSED*

From the time of their capture in Africa, through Emancipation and the Great Migration, to the national economic and housing crisis of today, people of African descent in the United States have been defined by their search for home. Using the dreams and aspirations of four families as her point of departure, Laura Gottesdiener narrates a beautifully crafted story about predatory lending, foreclosure abuse, the racial politics of home ownership, and the brave struggles launched by African American communities to keep their dignities and their homes. She demonstrates that amidst the greatest housing crisis the nation has seen, the current struggle among African Americans for economic equality is forcing upon our nation a redefinition of American freedom, one that challenges us to reconsider the fundamental flaw in our national security: the market-driven character of housing. With great humanity and solidarity for those on the front lines of this epic battle, Gottesdiener offers a compelling political analysis, and a way forward in a time of national crisis. *A Dream Foreclosed* is a powerful, impressive and page-turning testimony that ordinary people can fight back and win.

—JOHANNA FERNANDEZ, professor in the
Department of History at Baruch College

"*A Dream Foreclosed* finds beauty amidst immense pain and suffering—the beauty of people continuing to fight back against rapacious banks, the politicians they buy and the lawyers they hire. It is a work both beautiful and terrible that deserves to be read by many."

—MUMIA ABU-JAMAL, *Counterpunch*

"A remarkable book that hits hard against the big Wall Street banks"

—RUSSELL MOKHIBER, *Huffington Post*

A Dream Foreclosed is a poignant love letter to the best part of the "American Dream," which today lies in tatters amid the wreckage of the financial meltdown: the notion of a stable place to call home. Herein we are reminded not only of the human toll of this still-unfolding crisis, but the ways in which it stands as part of a longer drama, particularly for Black America, in which neither homeownership nor personhood itself have ever been finally secure, resting as both have on the shifting sands of political fate. A brilliant and needed narrative by an insightful and inspiring author.

—TIM WISE, author of several books including
Dear White America: Letter to a New Minority

The legislation to rescue the perpetrators of the current financial crisis included provisions for limited compensation to their victims. No need to tarry on which part of the bargain has been fulfilled. The bare statistics on foreclosures are shattering enough. But the enormity of the crime strikes home vividly in the heart-rending accounts of those who are brutally thrown out of their modest homes—for African Americans particularly, almost all they have—then survive in the streets, struggle on, and sometimes even regain something of what was stolen from them thanks to the courageous and inspiring work of the home liberation activists, now reinforced by the Occupy movement. All recounted with historical depth and analytic insight in this most valuable study.

—NOAM CHOMSKY

Americans need the stories in this book: inspiring resistance to the serialized corporate crimes that crush not only "Dreams" but the capacity to thrive beyond subsistence.

—LINN WASHINGTON, author of *Black Judges on Justice,*
Perspectives from the Bench

CONTENTS

The Fight

A Dream Deferred
by Langston Hughes

What happens to a dream deferred?
Does it dry up
like a raisin in the sun?
Or fester like a sore—
And then run?
Does it stink like rotten meat?
Or crust and sugar over—
like a syrupy sweet?

Maybe it just sags
like a heavy load.

Or does it explode?

Martin Luther King Jr., March 26, 1964. Photo by Marion S. Trikosko. (Library of Congress, Prints and Photographs Division)

FOREWORD

by Clarence Lusane

*Just as the doctrine of white supremacy came into being
to justify the profitable system of slavery, through shrewd
and subtle ways some realtors perpetuate the same racist
doctrine to justify the profitable real estate business.[1]*

—REV. MARTIN LUTHER KING JR.

Rev. Martin Luther King, at the time of his assassination, was on
the front lines of the fight for workers in Memphis and in the
process of launching a nationwide poor people's campaign. Few
recall that exactly one week after his murder, on April 11, 1968,
President Lyndon B. Johnson signed into law the Fair Housing
Act. The Act outlaws discrimination in the sale, rental, and
financing of dwellings, and in other housing-related transactions,
based on race, color, national origin, religion, sex, familial status,
or disability. This law, Title VIII of the Civil Rights Act of 1968,
honored the Herculean struggle waged by King for two years to
highlight the issue of housing segregation and discrimination.

In 1965, King brought the civil rights movement to the
North and took on the issue of open housing in Chicago and
its suburbs. At the time, Chicago was the second-largest city
in the United States, and its systems of education, employment,
and housing were as segregated as any in the deep South.

King hoped to release what he called an army of nonviolent protesters that would challenge these conditions and bring about fundamental change. However, he hit a solid wall of white—and often violent—opposition that involved elected officials, law enforcement authorities, bankers, real estate agents, lawyers, and ordinary citizens. As a result, legislation was stalled in Congress until the political opening caused by King's murder—and the widespread riots that followed—allowed Johnson to push the bill through in only a week.

Today, we see a more dressed-up but similar rogues' coalition, which, rather than prevent black homeownership, has figured out a way to exploit it. Instead of bottles and bricks thrown at protesters and marchers, the weapons of choice have been usurious mortgage contracts and signing pens. The language of segregation and interposition has been replaced with false narratives of getting a piece of the American pie and property ownership as freedom. The evil of "states' rights" has given way to the perniciousness of bankers' rights. For many families in the black community, home mortgages became new shackles, ending dreams and futures.

As Laura Gottesdiener documents in her brilliant discourse on the battle over home and community by African Americans, housing has always been integral to the fight for racial equality and justice. In a humane and somber voice, she captures the brutality of how those working in the political, real estate, banking, and financial sectors coordinate and collude to garner superprofits irrespective of the mass destruction caused to millions of individual mortgage holders or the nation's economic security as a whole. So egregious have their practices been that they triggered massive national and international losses, bringing global economies to the brink of collapse. This criminal enterprise, for which not a single banker or official in the financial or banking industry has yet to be prosecuted or imprisoned, has forced millions of American families out of their homes and into the streets. African American and Latino homeowners, in particular, have paid dearly, as they were disproportionately targeted and victimized by the predatory schemes and con games enacted by those devoid of any sense of national community or conscience.

As far back as 2006, the Center for Responsible Lending was already wary of the subprime loans targeting the black community. The Center predicted that unless the government intervened, it was likely that bankers would directly cause "the largest loss of African-American wealth that we have ever seen, wiping out a generation of home wealth building."[2]

Gottesdiener exposes how very deliberate, shocking strategies to target the black community were implemented. Black churches, rather than white ones, were seen as sites to heavily promote and market toxic loans. Real estate agents were given bonuses if they could convince black clients, regardless of their ability to carry the terms of the loan, to take the higher-cost, higher-risk deals. Shameless racism and financial predation were the order of the day throughout the entire home-financing industry.

The housing devastation experienced by the black community in the last few years is but one outrage in a context of unyielding economic turmoil. Many scholars and economists have lamented the disparate impact of the recession on black and Latino communities. As *Dollars & Sense* magazine noted, "The Great Recession produced the largest setback in racial wealth equality in the United States over the last quarter century."[3] Indeed, only halfway through the crisis, the "typical black household in 2009 was left with less wealth than at any time since 1984."[4] *CNN*

Money released a report in 2012 stating that not only is the median wealth of white households twenty times that of black households, but black wealth has undergone a devastating decline—53 percent from 2005 to 2009—with the result that the typical black household possessed less than $5,000 in wealth, compared to over $100,000 for whites.[5]

But the crisis that has eviscerated African American homeowners and potential homeowners is about much more than just profits and rapacious greed. Fundamentally, the battle is over community. For many African Americans, owning a home is about building a community and maintaining the stability that allow for active participation in one's neighborhood and in society more generally. The goal of owning a home has never been simply a pie-in-the-sky or abstract notion of the American Dream. It has been an indicator of individual achievement but also a collective accomplishment embedded in the struggle for racial equality, justice, and solidarity.

The four families profiled by Gottesdiener speak over and over again about their fear of losing community roots, an anxiety in some ways more terrifying than just the physical or economic loses they face. Detroit's Bertha Garrett speaks for them and many more when she states, "Memory lives in a space. This is what people don't understand. We raised our kids here. It's more than just an investment." To uproot a people is to uproot their culture, social networks, economic ties, and even spiritual bonds. The stories told by Garrett, Griggs Wimbley, Michael Hutchins, Martha Biggs, and too many others echo the narratives of refugees around the world who have been forced to search for a new home, new roots, new social and personal connections. In the lingua franca of the United Nations, the economic storm that swept the nation generated a humanitarian crisis consisting of millions of people internally displaced by foreclosure and eviction.

Like Dr. King, Gottesdiener also draws a link between two historic facts: that prior to the Civil War enslaved blacks were legally seen as "property"; and that following the Civil War, acquiring "property" was a considered a foundational need for a free people, a view that even the U.S. government held for a brief period during Reconstruction. The notion of people who were once "property" now owning property was a radical one that challenged long-held views about the place of African Americans in U.S. society. Historically, from sharecroppers' fields to urban ghettos, the struggle over land and home has embodied the complex dialogue between race and belonging. She quotes Professor Margalynne J. Armstrong, who states "African Americans have a relationship to property that differs from that of other Americans. Our introduction to this country was as a form of property, [and] contemporary relationships between African Americans and property are still impaired."

We owe Gottesdiener a great debt for her research and powerful argument in *A Dream Foreclosed*. There is a debate going on in the United States that few are aware of or acknowledge. That debate is over whether housing—clean, affordable, safe—should be seen as a fundamental human right. And, in fact, a host of international legal documents, many of which the U.S. government has signed and ratified, see it as such. Article 25 of the Universal Declaration of Human Rights states, "Everyone has the right to a standard of living adequate for the health and well-being of himself and of his family, including food, clothing, housing and medical care and necessary social services, and the right to security in the event of unemployment, sickness, disability, widowhood, old age or other lack of livelihood in circumstances beyond his control."[6]

Article 11 of the International Convention on Economic, Social and Cultural Rights declares, "The States Parties to the present Covenant recognize the right of everyone to an adequate standard of living for himself and his family, including adequate food, clothing and housing, and to the continuous improvement of living conditions."[7]

Fortunately, as Gottesdiener details and celebrates, the tale does not end with bankers simply getting away with visiting economic mass destruction on black America. The crisis has also given birth to an innovative and growing fightback across the nation. Above all, *A Dream Foreclosed* documents that a movement of resistance to the housing-as-profit thinking has reemerged and is challenging fundamental assumptions about the significance of home and community. Groups such as Take Back the Land, City Life/Vida Urbana, and others have stopped dislodgments, reversed evictions, and occupied territories in the name of protecting human rights. These acts of courage and conscience hearken back to the heroic campaigns of the 1930s that fought farm seizures and landlord abuses. Many forget or never knew that those battles eventually led to the development of progressive public housing policies in the United States.

While countless stories have been reported about the bursting of the housing bubble, the struggle for access to housing is rarely covered in the major media or even in the alternative press. Gottesdiener's effort here is a much needed and welcomed counterweight to the millstone of national silence. She takes sides in this battle and gives voice to those who are rarely, if ever, heard. *A Dream Foreclosed* takes up a question raised by Dr. King many years ago:

Now, in order to answer the question, "Where do we go from here?" which is our theme, we must first honestly recognize where we are now.... Let us be dissatisfied until slums are cast into the junk heaps of history, and every family will live in a decent, sanitary home. . . . But difficult and painful as it is, we must walk on in the days ahead with an audacious faith in the future.[8]

Martha Biggs takes a break looking out the window of the home for just a second. Although, Martha knows that any moment people could come to evict her family, she is still more afraid of having no place to go and subjecting her family to sleeping back in the family's minivan. Photo and caption by Brent Lewis.

INTRODUCTION

The search for justice, opportunity, and liberty that characterized the twentieth century for African Americans can be described as a quest for home. . . . Passion for home ran like a lifeblood through the African American psyche.

—VALERIE SWEENEY PRINCE, Burnin' Down the House: Home in African American Literature

The police were at the door.

Running footsteps on the stairs, and then—

"Martha Biggs! Ms. Biggs! Open up!" a man shouted.

Nine-year-old Jimmya Biggs remembers the pounding of fists followed by the deliberate thud of a battering ram. She and her seven-year-old sister Justice had just finished eating cereal, and they were playing Barbie in the living room of their two-family home on the West Side of Chicago. It was the weekend. Later that afternoon, Jimmya her two sisters planned to pick up their progress report cards from Salazar Elementary. Jimmya was a smart and well-behaved student, and she was excited to read her teachers' comments.

The pounding grew louder. The girls' older sister Jajuanna was still asleep on the middle level of the triple-layer bunk bed that the sisters shared. Jimmya peered out the window. Nearly a half dozen police cars were parked below. Their lights were flashing. The girls' mother, Martha Biggs, woke to the commotion and rushed to the door. She opened it, only to see seven police officers, a blinding flashlight, and her dreams exploding once again. It was 2010—the year that, for the first time in U.S. history, banks seized more than one million homes, evicting nearly three thousand families every single day.[9]

Martha yelled at the girls to get dressed. Jimmya and Justice flew into the bathroom together ("I was so scared—so, so, so, so scared!" Jimmya confided later). Martha and Jajuanna grabbed bags of clothes and ran down the stairs, shoving them into the family minivan. Martha had suspected that her landlord was in foreclosure when he'd stopped making repairs, and she'd already packed up some of their things. The girls emerged from the bathroom; a female police officer knelt down to remind Jimmya to put on a coat and shoes. Martha roused her only son, three-year-old Davion, and coaxed him into the car. The family fit, but it was tight: Martha and Jajuanna in the front seat, Jimmya, Justice, and Davion crowded between clothes and coats in the back. As Martha drove away from the house that had been their home and headed to Salazar Elementary School (the girls' report cards were good, as they'd hoped), Martha knew that this eviction was not only part of the 2008 housing crisis. It was part of a much longer story, one that stretched back to Martha's own childhood and even further, all the way back to the founding of the United States—a story of housing, race and freedom that weaves through the nation's history like the crisscross stitches on the fabric of a quilt.

Home. A place to live. The importance of this universal human need reverberates and ripples across the physical landscape of the United States and across the imagination of American society. To nineteenth-century author Anna Julia Cooper, who had been enslaved as a child and became one of the nation's leading intellectuals, a place to live is "not merely a house to shelter the body, but a home to sustain and freshen the mind."[10]

Home is an emotional place of promise and dreams. Getting there has been the subject of song, literature and myth dating back to the dawn of civilization. In the United States, the significance of a home has been central to notions of who we are and who we want to be. The living embodiment of the American Dream is to own a simple house with a white picket fence. "It's just a plain little old house—but it's made good and solid—and it will be *ours*," is how Mama explains the dream home in *A Raisin in the Sun*.[11]

An indecent place to live is a crowded space where dreams wither. As Gwendolyn Brooks writes in "Kitchenette Building," a poem about the subdivided apartments in 1960s African American neighborhoods:

We are things of dry hours and the involuntary plan,
Grayed in, and gray. "Dream" makes a giddy sound, not strong
Like "rent," "feeding a wife," "satisfying a man."

But could a dream sent up through onion fumes
Its white and violet, fight with fried potatoes
And yesterday's garbage ripening in the hall,
Flutter, or sing an aria down these rooms,

Even if we were willing to let it in,
Had time to warm it, keep it very clean,
Anticipate a message, let it begin?

We wonder. But not well! not for a minute!
Since Number Five is out of the bathroom now,
We think of lukewarm water, hope to get in it.[12]

And being without a place to live is one of the most traumatizing experiences in contemporary American society. As Jimmya explained two years after her family's eviction from her home on the West Side of Chicago: "When I was homeless, it wasn't like I was dirty, because my mom made sure I wasn't. But then I was going to school with everything on my mind of what happened the other night—that yesterday I got a house, but what about today? I might have to sleep in the car today. I might get a good meal today. But will I get a meal? Will something go wrong? What will happen? *How will I get home today?*"

Home is one of the most complicated words in the English language. According to *Webster's Dictionary*, the word home has six definitions, including:

The house in which one lives with his family

One's native land

A place of refuge and rest; the native and eternal dwelling place of the soul[13]

Home originates from the Anglo-Saxon word *ham*, which means "a village or town, an estate or possession."[14] Home continues to carry this dual meaning, signifying both community (village) and commodity (estate). The word house, often used as synonym for home, also carries these multiple definitions. "A house is, in all its figurings, always *thing, domain*, and *meaning—home, dwelling*, and *property*; *shelter, lodging*, and *equity*; *roof, protection*, and *aspiration*," write scholars Paula Chakravartty and Denise Ferreira da Silva.[15] While it is a small, humble word, the power of home is nearly unrivaled. It is the prize of epic heroes. It is where children are born and adults die. It is nearly synonymous with the idea of equality, upward mobility, and freedom. But it is also a word that, when misused, can unleash great destruction—including the worst financial collapse since the 1930s. As law professor Anita Hill writes, "At the heart of the crisis is the ideological disconnect between home as a basic element of the American Dream and pathway to equality, and home as a market product."[16]

The definition of home has legal, political, and economic consequences. Property (the estate) and personhood (the individual and her rights) have been interconnected since the dawn of the Western tradition. According to John Locke—called by one scholar the "ultimate Founding Father"[17]—even a person's connection to her or his own body is defined by property relations. "[E]very man has a property in his own person," Locke wrote in *The Second Treatise on Civil Government*.[18] This relation between property ownership and full personhood served as the legal foundation for the early U.S. Constitution, which granted only white, male property-holding individuals the right to political participation. Home and landownership gave one access to the original American Dream: democracy. As nineteenth-century philosopher G.W.F. Hegel wrote, "Property is the first embodiment of freedom."[19]

Property has also embodied the very opposite of freedom for a large number of people throughout the history of the United States. In the early United States, many communities suffered at the hands of the United States' particular version of property law, which hinged on rights of exclusion—*I own this; therefore, you have no right to it*—that were recognized only when the owner was a white man. This selective right to exclude was used by whites to control and disenfranchise Native Americans, African Americans, and Mexicans, who were rendered immigrants in their own lands by U.S. expansion. But the racism in U.S. property law did more than prohibit many from being owners. It determined who, in the eyes of the law and society, was considered a person. As law professor Margalynne J. Armstrong writes, "African Americans have a historical relationship to property that differs from that of other Americans. Our introduction to this country was *as a form of property* [and] contemporary relationships between African Americans and property are still impaired" (emphasis mine).[20]

The collapse of home—and home ownership—that began surfacing in late 2007 has created not only an economic disaster but a crisis in national identity. On the surface, this catastrophe is about the price of our houses. But more fundamentally, this ongoing crisis challenges the very foundation of American democracy. It is prompting us to question what it means to live in a society in which ownership is not only the dream but the underlying basis of full personhood. And it is forcing millions of Americans to experience for the first time how it feels to be on the wrong side of the property line.

The true scale of the crisis, which is still far from over, has not yet been fully understood. In human terms, an estimated ten million people have been forced out of their homes through foreclosure and bank eviction from 2007 to 2013.[21] *Ten million people.* That is more than thirty times the number of people who rushed to California in pursuit of gold in the 1850s. It is four times the number of people who fled the Dust Bowl in the 1930s. Even the Great Migration—the eighty-year march of Southern-born African Americans to Northern and Western cities during the twentieth century—involved only six million people. As a contemporary comparison, ten million is more than the number of people who currently live in all of Michigan, one of the most highly populated states in the union.[22] In other words, it's as if bankers have evicted and repossessed the homes of every man, woman, and child in the Great Lakes state.

In purely financial terms, the ongoing crisis and subsequent economic restructuring have cost unknown trillions of dollars. According to the U.S. Treasury Department, it has destroyed $19.2 trillion in U.S. household wealth, dragging millions deeper into debt and poverty.[23] The nation's primary economic engine of the last half century—the housing market—simply imploded. Multiple cities have declared bankruptcy. Homelessness among children under the age of seventeen in Florida has nearly doubled.[24] And, according to a Center for Responsible Lending report in 2011, "We are not even halfway through the foreclosure crisis."[25]

In the spring and summer of 2012, I drove across the country to study families and neighborhoods that were trying to stop foreclosure and displacement. As I witnessed inspiring stories and actions, I began observing something that took the project in an entirely unexpected direction. Through hundreds of interviews with families experiencing housing instability, I noticed that perceptions of the crisis were often influenced by race. White Americans often spoke about foreclosure as a singular, shocking event. Many blamed relatively recent changes in the U.S. economic structure, such as lending deregulation, the stagnation of middle-class wages or the development of the securitization process, which mortgage-pushing companies and Wall Street used to cash in on predatory, often unpayable loans. In contrast, African Americans rarely spoke about foreclosure as if it were something new and unprecedented, or even something that only affected mortgage-holding families.[26] Instead, they tied today's housing crisis to a longer fight for home—one that encompasses hundreds of years and includes everyone from families who pay mortgages to people who live in public housing. Most strikingly, they often proposed far more visionary economic and social solutions, sometimes even questioning the very fundamental structure of housing in America. When I mentioned my observations to Max Rameau, co-founder of the national housing network Take Back the Land, he agreed. "White people see this as a foreclosure problem. Black communities see this as part of a historic pattern of disenfranchisement," he said.

The ongoing foreclosure crisis has displaced and evicted families of every race and ethnicity. In fact, more white Americans have been forced from their homes since 2007 than people of any other racial or ethnic group.[27] Yet the nation hasn't evolved beyond the long legacy of racism in property relations. Black families and neighborhoods have been disproportionately victimized by bankers' predatory loans and illegal mortgage servicing practices.[28] Compared to white Americans, African Americans are twice as likely to be forced from their homes through bank-pursued eviction.[29] The Center for Responsible Lending estimates a full 25 percent of African American families who purchased new houses or refinanced mortgages during the height of the predatory lending frenzy could lose their homes before the crisis is over. Bankers' eviction and repossession of people's homes have already decimated some black communities; more than one-third of African American families in Detroit—a city that once had one of the highest Black homeownership rates in the nation— have already been forced out.[30] These statistics hold true across class lines. Lower-, middle-, and upper-class African American families have all been evicted from their homes at roughly the same rate.[31] Nor can the higher rates of foreclosure be explained by racial disparities in credit ratings.[32] The truth is that bankers' predatory targeting of people of color is one of the main reasons that millions of African Americans have lost their homes.

The full significance of these statistics, the reality they represent, has been startlingly unexamined. Because of the deep and enduring connection between property and personhood, today's ongoing wave of racially tilted displacement is part of a long history of denying full human and citizenship rights to African Americans and other people of color. It's a history, often suppressed or ignored, that began the moment Europeans set foot on North America and Africa, and continues to the present day. And most silenced of all is the story of the families who are organizing against this displacement, battling bankers, government officials, courts and the police to defend not only the places they live but also their very freedom. As Anita Hill writes, "nothing better represents the twisted path to racial and gender equality in America than the search for home."[33]

The contemporary chapter of this struggle began in the winter of 1865, four months before the end of the Civil War, in the abandoned rice fields of the Georgia and South Carolina coast. A fledgling society was emerging, complete with schools, courts, employment, and the promise of mass landownership for the freedmen.[34] The Thirteenth Amendment abolishing slavery had just been passed, and Union General William T. Sherman issued Field Order Fifteen, which declared that these eight hundred thousand acres of land were to be redistributed to the freedmen in forty-acre plots.[35] Land redistribution was central to the North's emancipation program—a recognition that land ownership was nearly synonymous with personhood in this era. As W.E.B. Dubois wrote in *The Souls of Black Folk*, "It has long been the more or less definitely expressed theory of the North that all the chief problems of Emancipation might be settled by establishing the slaves on the forfeited lands of their masters, a sort of poetic justice, said some."[36] But a mere six months later, President Andrew Johnson reversed General Sherman's order and the displacement began: The forty thousand men and women of color who had settled these fields, setting up their own system of government and commerce, were told that the land was to be returned to the white enslavers.

The decision to abandon land redistribution doomed the Reconstruction effort. The South established a new economy based on sharecropping and convict leasing, a system of near slavery in which white Americans owned all the land, and African Americans worked the fields for sums so paltry they would never be able to purchase plots of their own. Throughout the rest of the nineteenth century and into the twentieth, Black intellectual leaders debated questions of identity, nationalism, and economic uplift in a nation where, as Dubois wrote, the African American was "an outcast and a stranger in mine own house."[37] According to Jonathan Holloway, professor of African American history at Yale University, these conversations and debates were "all about claiming a home in a sense." Meanwhile, millions of African Americans oppressed by the rural South's Jim Crow laws and apartheid economy quietly embodied this struggle with their feet: fleeing the South and seeking new homes in Western, Northern, and even some major Southern cities. As the Great Migration began in earnest, the pursuit of freedom, full personhood, and home through journey became, as Toni Morrison said, "one of the monumental themes" in African American literature.[38]

Yet, as people boarded trains by the carful and cities flourished under the jazz beat of the Harlem Renaissance, many realized that there is a thin line between journey and displacement. African American literature began to echo with what August Wilson, author of the Pulitzer Prize-winning play *Fences*, called "the walking blues."[39] Ralph Ellison captured this psychological dislocation in *Invisible Man*, an epic novel of the narrator's journey through 1930s Harlem whose very title testifies to the lack of personhood that is a condition of constant motion and displacement.[40] At the end of the novel, Ellison's unnamed narrator is driven underground, while—aboveground and in real life—intense housing and lending discrimination drove many African Americans into overcrowded and impoverished sections of cities. The homeownership rate for white Americans exploded after World War II, thanks to the Federal Housing Administration's extensive whites-only lending program and the expansion of suburbs with racially restrictive covenants. But African Americans and other people of color were barred, once again, from these homes and their freedoms. Home became the dream deferred.

Once again, African Americans fought back. The Civil Rights era ushered in massive political and social organizing to desegregate and heal a racially fractured society. Challenging property relations and housing discrimination was central to the struggle for full, effective citizenship. As Stokely Carmichael wrote, "Black Americans are a propertyless people in a country where property is valued above all. We had to work for power, because this country does not function by morality, love, and nonviolence, but by power."[41] Through decades of block-by-block organizing, the Black community defeated the majority of explicitly racist housing and lending laws. Legally, this movement culminated in the passage of the Fair Housing Act in 1968 and the Community Reinvestment Act in 1977—legislation that was supposed to end housing and lending discrimination.

But a new narrative about homes and the American Dream soon emerged—propagated not only by industry but also by the

White House. It was the home's *equity* that promised freedom and full personhood—not the home itself. As President George W. Bush declared at the 2002 White House Conference on Minority Homeownership, "All of us here in America should believe, and I think we do, that we should be, as I mentioned, a nation of owners. Owning something is freedom, as far as I'm concerned. . . . It's a part of an asset-based society."[42] This wealth-as-freedom narrative that was pitched so aggressively to African Americans was never about achieving universal rights, social justice, or equality. Instead, it was part of the advertising to lure new consumers to bankers who sold the idea of owning a home while binding millions of Americans, particularly those of color, to a life of unpayable debts. And when the bubble burst, all those Americans' dreams—so close to realization, it seemed—became the living nightmares of eviction, destroyed credit, and life as "an outcast and a stranger" in their homeland.

Today, Black America continues to fight for a place to call home. From grassy fields to postindustrial plains, from river-cradled towns to brick-faced cities, a movement is brewing. Block by block, a sense of resistance is taking root in Black communities—one that is informed by this racial history and defined by the growing conviction that there *must* be a better way to live in America. But don't be mistaken: This is not a movement to increase African Americans' access and opportunities in the current housing market. Instead, like past Black-led movements, today's uprising seeks to change the very economic and social system itself—to replace this model with one that is built on ideals of equality and community.

This book voices some of the life histories of four people who are part of this struggle: Griggs Wimbley in Sanford, North Carolina; Bertha Garrett in Detroit, Michigan; Michael Hutchins in Chattanooga, Tennessee; and Martha Biggs in Chicago,

Illinois. In the first section, "The Dream," these four individuals search throughout the 1990s for new homes in a larger pursuit for happiness, familial security, independence, or basic survival. In the second section, "The Explosion," they find themselves and their homes under attack in the 2000s, threatened by bankers, politicians and a society in crisis. Finally, in "The Fight," all four refuse to abandon their dreams, and they embark on new, seemingly impossible journeys that pit them against the most powerful force in human history: modern capitalism.

Although these stories span only three decades, they are part of a much longer history: the epic quest of African Americans to make a home in a nation that has, for too many centuries, proven an inhospitable land. But in some ways, these stories have nothing to do with race at all. For these individuals are doing what people throughout history have always done when their most sacred dreams are threatened by evil or injustice.

They fight back.

THE DREAM

When you sign papers on the mortgage,
that's the American Dream.

To own a place and call it your home.

—*Bertha Garrett, Detroit*

There's this 'American Dream,' but I'm not
even looking for a dream. I'm just looking for
sustenance."

—*Rob Robinson, New York City*

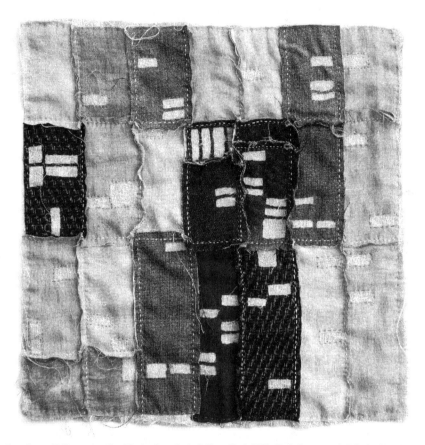

Foreclosure Quilt representing Atlanta, Georgia, by Kathryn Clark, 2011. Made from recycled denim, bleached linen, yarn and embroidery thread, 19.5" x 19.5". Foreclosures shown in rectangles stitched in light thread.

My previous work as an urban planner made me acutely aware of how big an impact the foreclosure crisis would have on our cities and towns throughout the United States. However, very little was mentioned in the news. It was important to me to present the whole story in a way that would captivate people's attention and make a memorable statement. Making map quilts seemed an ironic solution. Quilts act as a functional memory, an historical record of difficult times. It is during times of hardship that people have traditionally made quilts, often resorting to scraps of cloth when so poor they could not afford to waste a single thread of fabric.

The neighborhoods shown are not an anomaly; they are a recurring pattern seen from coast to coast, urban to suburban neighborhoods across the United States. The problem has not been solved, it is still occurring, just changing shape, affecting more of us.

—Kathryn Clark

ONE HUNDRED ACRES OF HOUSES

Griggs Wimbley
Sanford, North Carolina

The field was bursting with promise and opportunity. Griggs Wimbley could see it from his own small lot at the base of Tempting Church Road: one hundred acres of untouched land. Covered with North Carolina grass, the plot began behind the church across the road and stretched all the way to the small dirt path by the corner store on the way to town. Griggs had been born on this road, a few lots away from where he now lived. He'd been looking at this land nearly all his life.

The property was jointly owned by seven brothers and sisters, but they hadn't done anything with it. Griggs, on the other hand, had plans. When he looked at that expansive plot, he saw a dream: a field of houses.

"One hundred acres of land—can you imagine how many houses?" he said later. "I saw a vision, such a beautiful thing. I love horses; there was going to be horses outside. It was going to be one pretty place. You come down there, you were going to move there. . . . All I wanted to do was to build houses to help people have a place to live."

It was the late 1980s when Griggs first dreamed of dotting the land with pretty white homes, backyards, and horses. At the time, he lived with his new wife in a small brown trailer, working landscaping and remodeling during the day and data processing at Central Carolina Hospital at night. His wife, Audrey, also worked at Central, in the laboratory. Griggs had studied business in college, and he had an ambitious, entrepreneurial mind. He'd been the first African American student in Lee County Senior High School's accelerated classes. Reading didn't do much for him, but he had a way with numbers. And he could build just about anything he set his mind to.

Tempting Church Road was a humble, old-fashioned place six miles outside the small town of Sanford, North Carolina. But a great change was sweeping rural parts of the country, and Griggs recognized the moment. Like centuries of Americans before him, he saw the grassy field as an opportunity for expansion, wealth and growth. He had his own dream: He would buy those one hundred acres and populate them with perfect, cookie-cut suburban houses.

Like Griggs's, the American Dream began with land.

"We have opened the fertile plains of the Ohio to the poor, the needy, and the oppressed of the Earth," George Washington boasted in a 1785 letter. "Anyone therefore who is heavy laden or who wants land to cultivate, may repair thither & abound as in the Land of promise, with milk and honey."[43]

In Washington's time, this promise didn't include African Americans, native peoples or anyone besides chosen whites. Barred from owning land or voting, Griggs's ancestors were, legally speaking, considered more as parcels of property than as potential landholders. But two hundred years later, Griggs had been told that the country had changed, that he too could carve out a small Promised Land down in rural North Carolina. Itching to get himself and his wife out of their trailer, Griggs purchased a seven-acre tract of land a little farther down Tempting Church Road. It cost $13,000, which he began paying off with $200 checks every week.

Griggs built his and Audrey's new home by hand. He poured the foundation, laid the bricks, snaked the wiring through the walls. He added luxuries, too: a skylight in the roof and a spiral staircase winding down to the furnished basement. For decades he dreamed of building a porch swing where he and Audrey could sit. He eventually found a wooden one at a yard sale and installed it.

Sanford, North Carolina, was a place where the stately old houses were built with brick. First an agricultural, enslavers' economy, the region switched to manufacturing and developed into the "Brick Capital of the World" after the Civil War. Sawmills and brickyards sprang up throughout the twentieth century, but the area and its culture remained rural.

Lewis Hooker, a member of Griggs's extended family, remembers buying his first gun in 1967.

"My daddy permitted me to walk into Sanford to a place called Hester and Wilson . . . I wrote a check for the gun, the shells, the vest—the whole nine yards. And walked out of town at fourteen with a gun on my shoulder."

Tempting Church Road was named after Tempting Congregation, a small church house that loomed over the middle of the street. The street's culture was religious and traditional, but Griggs could feel that something else was in store for Sanford. City folk had begun to move farther out, settling in Sanford and commuting fifty minutes into Raleigh or even an hour and fifteen minutes into Durham for their jobs at biotech companies downtown. As Griggs predicted, the whole county's population would explode, increasing almost 40 percent from 1990 to 2010.[44]

It was a phenomenon repeating itself across the country, an expansion emanating from the urban cores that was turning rural land into suburban communities. To some on the edge, it was an invasion. One farmer in rural Minnesota, about an hour from Minneapolis, posted a desperate sign on the edge of his property declaring, THIS IS STILL A FARM . . . WITH LIVE ANIMALS . . . NOT FOR SALE!

But to others, like Griggs, it was an opportunity. He began

studying the business of modular home construction, sending away for catalogs filled with descriptions of the easy-to-assemble houses that could fill those one hundred acres.

"Anything you see, I could have ordered it," he said flipping through one company's catalog, which he had held on to for two decades.

The modular homes it featured, with elite, Anglo-Saxon names like "The Hamilton" and "The Franklin," transformed the American landscape and way of life. Made possible by the automobile and the United States' unparalleled manufacturing industry, construction and suburbanization exploded in post-World War II America.

If homeownership was the dream, then it was one that private industry had figured out how to mass produce and mass market for spectacular profits. As early as the 1930s, a coalition of industries—including real estate, insurance, timber, manufacturing, auto, oil, and finance—coalesced into a powerful lobbying force. Its goal: the expansion of a homeownership-based private housing industry. The state and federal government underwrote suburbanization through legislation and subsidies, particularly the National Housing Act of 1934, which created the Federal Housing Administration (FHA) and the quasi-governmental lending agencies Fannie Mae and Freddie Mac (the Federal National Mortgage Association and the Federal Home Loan Mortgage Corporation, respectively). Other legislation included the Federal Home Loan Bank Act, the Federal Highway Act, and homeowner entitlement programs, such as the mortgage-interest tax deduction. The government also helped ideologically. For example, Secretary of Commerce Herbert Hoover partnered with the real estate industry's lobbyist to create a pro-homeownership advertising "nonprofit," Better Homes for America, Inc., that marketed the home as the symbol of the American dream.[45]

With this legislation and propaganda in place, the homeownership rate soared during the second half of the twentieth century, rising from its historically stable level of 45 percent to nearly 70 percent by 2006.[46] Throughout this period, the increase in homeownership was driven by leveraged capital, also known as debt-financing: borrowing huge sums of money in the form of home mortgages, which carried interest rates and used the property itself as collateral. By 2008, the leveraging of the United States economy, particularly the mortgage industry, created the worst global crisis since the Great Depression.

But in the late 1990s when Griggs imagined his field of houses, there seemed to be no threat of crisis on the horizon. House prices rose annually, almost without fail. He and Audrey had strong credit, and together they earned between $70,000 and $80,000 a year. Griggs was in negotiations with the family that owned the one hundred acres; he already had architects drafting potential plans for the subdivision. And meanwhile, he kept on building the couple's future home, brick by brick.

Griggs was moving up. So he wasn't worried when, one afternoon in 1997, a salesman from First Greensboro Home Equity visited Griggs's half-finished future home and pitched him a construction loan. Griggs had originally planned to pay for the house as he built it, financing the construction through his and his wife's paychecks. But a loan would speed up the project so he could focus on the one hundred acres, he thought to himself. After all, he didn't just want to build a home for himself; he wanted to create that dream for other people, too.

The salesman offered Griggs terms for a $100,000 loan. The interest rate was high, but the salesman was insistent: In a few years, you can just refinance, he said.

Life was going so well, Griggs saw no reason not to accept the offer.

THE HOUSE IN THE WRONG PART OF TOWN

Bertha Garrett
Detroit, Michigan

The house was in the wrong part of town, and William Garrett knew it. A middle-aged barber with his own salon, William had sized up the house on Pierson Street in far Northwest Detroit. It was a dark brick single-story home, with a pitched shingled roof and small square windows. The front of the house was set back and angled away from the street. It looked hand built, like the majority of houses on the street. The neighborhood seemed quiet, though it looked a little rough around the edges. But the best part was the house's yard: a full 1.2 acres, big enough for the gardens and family parties that his wife, Bertha, loved so much. The only thing was, how could he convince Bertha, whom he feared would dislike the neighborhood? He knew how stubborn she could be, and he knew that if he went about it wrong, they might just spend the rest of their lives in that stupid little subdivision downtown.

Foolishly, William decided to try to outwit his wife. He coaxed her into the car in the middle of the night and drove her out to Pierson Street, hoping the cover of darkness would obscure the distance and the block. He wanted her to fall in love with the house before the neighborhood scared her away. The move was conniving, but can anyone blame him? It was 1990 and William was a grown man, a successful professional, itching for a home of his own.

The next day, Bertha called her eldest daughter, Michelle, who already lived on her own.

"Your Dad thinks he's slick," she told her daughter.

Nothing got past Bertha Garrett.

An elegant and deeply religious woman, Bertha grew up running through the backwoods of Alabama. Her father had been a farmer, and she loved wandering through the tiny trails behind their land as she picked through the underbrush. In Bertha's world, land was something that men toiled over and yearned for. For decades her father had tamed the fields, but when his daughter went back for a visit, years after she had migrated to Detroit, her homeland had once again become wild.

"My father stopped farming," she remembers. "So the animals had taken over the path. The animals know when humans are no longer here."

Bertha knew that her husband also wanted land. They were both cramped and crowded in their downtown subdivision, a place where families rented small subsidized houses with the assistance of a federal program called "Section 8." Although Michelle was grown, they had three young children in the house—and maybe, if they were lucky, more on the way. Bertha missed the land and nature. She loved flowers and gardening; they reminded her of Alabama.

Despite her husband's fears, Bertha was taken with the house and its surroundings on Northwest Pierson Street. The neighborhood was a solid, middle-class community. Across the street from the house that Bertha and William wanted lived an electrician; on their right was a paralegal. But something more powerful than class tied this block together. The neighborhood was an "enclave from the South," as Bertha describes it. The majority of the block's residents were, like Bertha and William, middle-class, Alabama-born African Americans who had fled north throughout the twentieth century as part of a massive movement called the

Great Migration. Inspired by visions of freedom from Jim Crow, safety from the racial violence, and jobs that paid dollars rather than cents, six million African Americans journeyed north in what is perhaps the greatest dream-fueled migration in U.S. history. It was more than just a physical movement. It was also, as Pulitzer Prize-winning journalist Isabel Wilkerson explains, a collective, psychological liberation through migration—"the first big step the nation's servant class ever took without asking."[47]

Tens of thousands of Southern-born African Americans came to Detroit during World War II, when the city was literally bursting with well-paying manufacturing jobs. For many Southerners at that time, Detroit was a legendary, even mythical, city, a place where massive factories churned out planes and guns at all hours of the day and night, and there were so many jobs that newcomers tripped over them the minute they stepped off the train platform.[48]

As new residents settled into the city during the 1940s and 1950s, racial tensions inscribed physical lines and divisions into the city's landscape that are still apparent today. The Federal Housing Administration (FHA) had the policy of redlining African American neighborhoods, meaning that the agency literally took maps of the United States and drew red lines around minority neighborhoods to mark where the government would not lend to families seeking a mortgage. Even white neighborhoods bordering the redlined areas were suspect, since the FHA worried that the areas might soon fall victim to "infiltration of inharmonious racial or nationality groups."[49]

As Yale University urban studies professor Dolores Hayden explains in *Building Suburbia*, Detroit is home to one of the nation's most iconic examples of housing segregation: a physical, concrete wall erected in 1940 to protect a white-only community. Initially, the FHA had refused to lend to the developer because his proposed subdivision bordered on an African American neighborhood. Only after he proposed building a six-foot-high concrete wall "running for a half-mile on the property line separating the black and white neighborhoods" did the government agree to provide federal loans and mortgage guarantees.[50]

Although physical walls were uncommon, this type of purposeful racial segregation, enforced by the federal government, was the norm in the housing industry throughout the majority of the twentieth century.

"A place like Levittown that made the dream of homeownership accessible to working-class families explicitly excluded Blacks," housing scholar Chris Bonastia said in an interview, referring to Levittown, New York, one of the largest planned suburbs in the nation, which houses more than fifty thousand people and prohibited all non-white residents until 1960.[51]

The economics of home prices incentivized segregation and even racial violence, Bonastia explained, because the value of properties plummeted when neighborhoods became integrated. And the Federal Housing Administration, as the nation's largest mortgage insurer, was often the driving force behind the segregation.[52]

"The Federal Housing Administration was a conservative business, especially racially," explained Bonastia. "It saw itself as an ally to the private sector, and what it did was based on the stamp of approval from private industry."

In other words, if a concrete wall was what the market demanded, it was what the FHA required.

The home that Bertha and William hoped to buy was only a few miles away from this iconic wall, but Bertha wasn't put off by the fact that the house was on the "wrong side" of town. She was well accustomed to the city's racialized nature. She'd arrived during the riots of 1967 and 1968, and throughout her decades in Detroit she'd watched the white residents' steady, anxious flight to the suburbs.

Yes, Bertha was quite taken with the neighborhood. There was only one problem: The house itself was not for sale.

The home's owner was a stubborn and eccentric writer named Ms. Ween. She was very possessive of the house because she and her husband had built it by hand in 1951. They had laid the bricks, dug up the yard, and planted an apple orchard and mulberry trees. The Weens had built it because African Americans hoping to buy their own home in the 1940s and 1950s had few options. The majority of lending came from the FHA, which refused to extend mortgages to them. Some took out predatory, secondary-market mortgages from loan sharks, so named because they preyed upon African American families by selling them loans with marked-up interest rates and a never-ending list of tacked-on fees. Others, like the Weens, bought land and built their homes themselves.

After her husband died, Ms. Ween vowed she would never leave her home, because it was filled with memories of her husband. She never put the house on the market. And even though she knew she would have to move eventually, neighbors worried that she'd never find a family that would make her satisfied enough to sell.

"She and her husband built this home and put the driveway in themselves," remembers Willie McDade, one of Bertha's neighbors and friends. "Ms. Ween was very particular about who would move into this home after she moved. . . . She promised us that she would sell this home to someone who was worthy and would take care of it, and she kept her word," said McDade.[53]

Bertha and William Garrett visited the house again, this time during daylight and with their baby son in tow. Ms. Ween fell in love with the little child. She offered to sell them the house.

William remembers feeling filled with pride that day, knowing that he, a barbershop owner and soon-to-be father of six, could afford to buy a house.

"I bought this house with the kind of money I made with six kids. She fell in love with one of my kids, and she told me she wanted me to have it. And I got it—she gave it to me—at a price I could afford to pay. So I just been proud and I'm happy to live here."[54]

Bertha, too, remembers the move as being filled with joy.

"This area was so beautiful when I first moved here," remembers Bertha.

And so the Garretts arrived, leaving the paintings and trinkets and yellowed pages of Ms. Ween's poetry untouched.

Over their twenty-two years in the home on Pierson Street, Bertha and William raised their children and grandchildren. The elegant living room and large backyard was the place for family dinners, picnics and graduation celebrations—from elementary school all way through a master's program. The backyard hosted three family weddings. For Michelle's in 1994, Bertha bent over with her pregnant belly and dug a pond in the backyard. Flower beds ringed the front lawn, and Ms. Ween's trees flourished and bore fruit. Every so often, the old woman would call Bertha to see how her mulberry tree was faring, and how old that beautiful baby boy was now.

That boy and the rest of Bertha's sons grew into pastors and deacons. Soon, the house became a refuge for eighteen grandchildren, who camped out in tents for two weeks each summer during Bertha's annual "Grandma and Grandpa Camp." Bertha would hire a horse to give the kids rides while her children gratefully enjoyed their kid-free vacations.

Herself a writer, Bertha found her favorite room was the library. She woke early, drank cup upon cup of tea, and sat among the books and heavy wood shelves reading the Bible and writing her own religious reflections before anyone else had roused. Later, she would give up the tea for Lent, thinking it might be an excess. She penned and published two books in that room, *Pushing Through the Crowd with Faith* and *Discipline Your Life to Serve a Risen Lord*. As she grew older, she retained her grace and the Southern lilt of her voice. Her skin was light and almost wrinkle-free, and her square jaw gave her a resolved, pensive look. She dressed properly, especially for church, donning outfits like a pressed white suit with prim ruffles, an embroidered muslin shawl, a cream-color smock and a large-brimmed white Southern hat. She might be living in postindustrial Detroit, but her home was a refuge, a sanctuary over which she had full control.

The mulberry tree and the summer camps, the horses and the verses, the children and the grandchildren—this was Bertha's life, and it was all contained in this house in the quiet neighborhood that was too far north and too far west. It was a swirling mix of chaos and calm, dinners and dishes, that reigns every day in millions of homes across the United States.

"Memory lives in a space," Bertha said. "This is what people don't understand. We raised our kids here. It's more than just an investment."

Hers are words that echo in living rooms across the country—a promise of comfort and stability that drove the frenzied rise in homeownership.

"This is our paradise," said Pamela Douglass, a woman in rural Minnesota. "We got married in this backyard, and so did our daughter."

For mothers especially, a safe and stable home is not an entrepreneurial or economic calculation; it is an intensely personal dream that can often feel like a woman's duty.

"I moved [to the suburbs] with a grand vision of saving my kids," recalled one mother who left Washington, D.C., to settle in North Carolina. Another described her home as the culmination of "hoping and praying that the American Dream could come to a single mother who ... decided to be responsible, pay bills, and try to get a house by thirty."

Housing activist Anthony Newby explained in an interview that, more than equity or investment, homeownership represents stability, family and future—particularly in the African American community.

"All people fundamentally really care about, speaking specifically to African Americans but also to the larger population, is knowing you can come to the place you've chosen to live, be able to afford it, and not be under threat," he said.

As Bertha settled into her new home in the early 1990s, she understood that her homemaking was part of this greater trend, this larger collective achievement that was swelling, expanding, and, for a fleeting moment, utterly magical.

"All the teachers, window washers, publishers, writers, garbage collectors, union workers, all the workers—when a man or a woman comes home after a day of work, there's a peacefulness," she said.

This was Bertha's definition of the American Dream: a peaceful place to come home to. But there was another story, a competing narrative of what homes are worth, that would soon come to threaten her own.

THE BOY WHO WAS FAST

Michael Hutchins
Chattanooga, Tennessee

For months, the only thing Michael Hutchins could do was dream. He couldn't walk. He couldn't speak. He couldn't care for himself. The skinny twenty-one-year-old simply lay in the Hamilton County nursing home in Chattanooga, Tennessee, trapped in a body that could perform none of the simple, day-to-day activities he longed to do.

The accident happened on December 31, 1992—the day of New Year's Eve. Michael was standing on the sidewalk on Baley Avenue just across the street from his mother's house. A speeding car jumped the curb and slammed into him. His smashed body was thrown through the air and landed a whole front yard away from where he'd been struck.

First Michael was rushed to Erlanger Hospital, where he lay in a coma for weeks. One afternoon, the man who had driven into Michael came to visit. When he saw the mangled face of the boy whose body had shattered his windshield, he burst into tears.

After Michael had been in a coma for a month, the doctors at Erlanger Hospital transferred him to the nursing home, "just for care," said his mother. He remained unconscious for another month, then two.

"They had really given Michael up to die," remembers his mother, Hattie.

Until one day, Michael opened his eyes.

"I didn't know where I was," said Michael. "I remember trying to get up out of the hospital bed, and I was hanging on for dear life. I was hooked up to all these tubes. That's about as far as my memory goes," said Michael.

He was awake, but he wasn't back; this wasn't the Michael from before the accident. As he lay in the nursing home, his mind wandered—dreaming about who he had been and wondering who he could still be.

Michael Hutchins had been a runner. The gangly young teenager with close-cropped hair took inspiration from his uncle, Howard Akins, who had been a famed runner in the family and who first encouraged Michael to stretch his legs. When Michael discovered the speed bottled up in his body, he joined the track team at Richard Hardy Junior High School. The school was right around the corner from Harriet Tubman Homes, Chattanooga's largest public housing project, where Michael lived with his mother, older brother, and nephew.

To those who didn't know Michael, those who had just seen him as a skinny young boy running through the streets around the neighborhood in Chattanooga, Michael might have been just another boy from the projects. But those close to him knew otherwise.

"If you talk to people that really know him," said his younger cousin, Jamaine Akins, "Michael was going to go do something, and be somebody. . . . You could tell by his attitude. You could just tell that he was always positive, he was always outgoing, he was always a go-getter."

The year Michael turned 11, the Harriet Tubman Homes had the worst crime rate in the entire city. One of his earliest memories of the place was witnessing two young boys get shot in his family's backyard. But Michael was quiet and caring, like his mother, who cared for two- and three-year-old children at a day-care center, and he never got involved in gangs or crime.

Instead, Michael often headed to his uncle's house after school, where he played football and wrestled with his younger cousins. The children worshipped him, recalls Jamaine Akins, although they wouldn't dare admit it.

As a teenager, Michael ran for his high school, Howard School of Academics and Technology, where he hit his stride as a middle-long-distance runner. In the fall he ran cross country; in the spring, track. In competitions, he ran as many events as his legs could bear, sometimes racing almost four miles throughout the course of four events: 400 meters, 800 meters, mile relay, and two-mile relay. Before each race, he jogged to the start line with confidence, shaking out his shoulders and arms to warm up. His mother, Hattie, often attended his meets, and she remembers that Michael always wore a faint smile on his lips. She frequently watched her son win ribbons and trophies, which he presented to her for safekeeping after the races.

The one thing that was challenging for Michael was his schoolwork.

"I wasn't a class clown, but school wasn't my thing," he remembers. At the time of Michael's enrollment, Howard was one of the worst schools in the state. When the federal government began tracking high school graduation rates, it found that only 30 percent of all students at Howard High ended up with a diploma.[55] But unlike the majority of his classmates, Michael was determined to finish, and he graduated on time with a reputation as a good-natured, independent young man who was headed somewhere fast.

A photo from the spring of 1988 captures Michael's life before the accident. Snapped just after Michael helped Howard High achieve a fourth-place finish at the regional competition, the photo shows a skinny boy and his teammates, Michael staring at the camera with the intensity of a young man with dreams.

But when Michael came out of the coma, he realized that everything had changed. Brain damage slowed life down. His memory was missing; words kept disappearing. He couldn't keep his right arm from shaking. Michael couldn't even remember how to walk, let alone run.

The doctors taught him sign language and how to take steps. After six months in the nursing home, his mother brought him home to live with her. A year passed, then another. He began to speak. His voice came out in a high, playful pitch, but he had to hunt through his halting memory for his every word.

To everyone's surprise, what he began talking about as he lay recovering in his mother's house was living on his own.

"Here I am, I was twenty-three, and I was thinking, I can't live like that," remembers Michael. He knew he'd lost something in the accident. "If it didn't happen, ain't no telling who I could have been," he said. But he wasn't going to allow the accident to take away the most important thing: his self-sufficiency.

The topic came as a shock for most of his family.

"No, no, no, we didn't expect that," said his cousin, Akins. We didn't know what to expect. Because that situation was really bad. . . . So I didn't expect him to try to be independent. I didn't even know what to expect."

But Hettie recognized her son's words; they were the same ones he'd been saying since he was a young, surprisingly independent teenager.

"That's what he was going to do before he had the accident, so he said he wanted to still try to get his own place," she said.

In a country centered on individualism, living on one's own has evolved into the very definition of freedom. This idea began as early as the Pilgrims, who associated their settlements with religious liberties. Nineteenth-century homesteading reinforced the self-reliance of living on one's own since, in that day, one could claim land in the West merely by working on it. Many early American writers, such as Henry David Thoreau and Ralph Waldo Emerson, inscribed self-reliance and individualism as transcendent American values. And the house always seemed to be the place where men and women found this personal freedom. In Harriet Beecher Stowe's classic novel, the cabin is the symbol of Uncle Tom's emancipation. For Virginia Woolf, the peaceful quiet of *A Room of One's Own* is the key to women's liberation.

As Walt Whitman wrote, "A man is not a whole and complete man unless he owns a house and the ground it stands on."[56]

And so, as Michael lay in his mother's house dreaming about a place of his own, he was yearning not for privacy or extra space. He was trying to prove himself, to recover his self-worth. In a sense, he was trying to become American.

Michael knew there was no way that he would be able to mortgage his own house. He received a small stipend each month in disability payments, not enough even to rent a one-bedroom apartment. Yet, as long as he saved his money carefully and spent very little, he could afford the sliding-scale cost of living in public housing.

Few today recognize public housing as a step towards independence. For the majority of Americans, the much maligned program represents the very opposite of self-reliance. But for millions of people, public housing has indeed represented a path toward independence and personal freedom that many like Michael couldn't find anywhere else in the country's for-profit housing market.

With his mother's help, Michel applied for an apartment through the Chattanooga Housing Authority, the city's public housing agency. His mother was worried; her son was still learning how to walk and talk, after all. No one had expected Michael to try to live on his own. The doctor's hadn't even expected him to regain consciousness.

But by the time Michael reached twenty-five, he had become adamant. When he got out there, out in the real world, he would *find* a way to make it work, he told his mother. They submitted a housing application and began to wait. As in almost every other urban center, public housing was in high demand and short supply—even before the frenzied decade of demolition that began in the late 1990s. Months passed. Finally, he received a phone call from the Chattanooga Housing Authority saying that space had opened up in the Westside, a neighborhood downtown filled with public housing developments.

"When I got the call that the Westside was ready, I was ready too," remembers Michael.

He was offered an apartment in a Westside development called College Hill Courts. Michael was both excited and apprehensive. Like millions of other young men and women, he saw the whole world stretched out before him, and he ached to join it, to become as independent as the nation expected him to be.

AS GOOD AS RATS

Martha Biggs and Jajuanna Walker
Chicago, Illinois

Everything was everywhere. That was how Jajuanna, Martha Biggs's oldest daughter, describes her life.

Jajuanna was five the year that she and Martha moved across the hall to apartment 837 in one of Cabrini Green's high-rise towers. The two-bedroom apartment was already crowded with women before Martha Biggs and her children moved in. Jajuanna's three older cousins, Janie, Christina, and Victoria, lived there, as well as Victoria's daughter. So did Jajuanna's godmother, Ke'Ana, and her daughter Tia. With Jajuanna and her mother, there was a total of eight women. When Jajuanna's younger sister Jimmya was born a few years later, that made nine.

People slept all over the place. Martha portioned off part of the living room with a curtain and created a makeshift bedroom where Jajuanna, Tia and then Jimmya all shared a bunk bed. Jajuanna remembers that there were a lot of arguments among the adults that she didn't understand. Neither was she paying them a lot of attention; she mostly spent her time thinking about whether she and her friends would be allowed to go outside. There was a garden at the intersection of North Hudson Avenue and Chicago Avenue where she and her sisters loved to plant tomatoes and make salads. Jajuanna remembers summer days when she and her sisters turned on the water spigot outside and their mother grabbed the hose, splashing children and neighbors whether they were ready to get wet or not.

Jajuanna's mother, Martha, was as tall and broad as most men, with helter-skelter front teeth and the high cheekbones that pass from generation to generation of Biggs women. Martha inherited them from her own mother, who migrated to Chicago from Jackson, Mississippi, as part of the same Great Migration that carried Bertha Garrett to Detroit. In Chicago, the movement's influx was so intense that at times ten thousand new residents a month joined the city's population.[57]

The other quality that runs in the Biggs women's blood is pride. One of Martha's favorite stories about her mother is that she caused a scandal by attending her husband's funeral dressed head to toe in red, because the promiscuous man had left her years earlier. She passed this self-respect to Martha, who was so proud she once refused to walk through the side door of a friend's house. ("I'm not a slave no more," she joked in her low, raspy voice.) The woman lived to see Martha pass these traits on to her firstborn daughter, Jajuanna Walker. Then, when Martha Biggs was only eighteen, her mother died.

The world Martha inherited as an orphan and a young teenage mother was Cabrini Green, the most infamous housing project in the United States. To nonresidents, this complex of high-rises and row houses that held a staggering twenty-five thousand people was outside the fabric of American society. It was spoken about only in hyperbole and hysteria: "a virtual war zone, the kind of place where little boys were gunned down on their way to school and little girls were sexually assaulted and left for dead in stairwells," cried an Associated Press article in 2010.[58]

But to Martha Biggs and her young daughter, Cabrini was a community filled with loyalty, passed-down clothes, and pooled food stamps. For the children, there were spelling bees and science fairs and the annual summer Cabrini Olympics, complete with ribbons and trophies. Churches donated pens and notebooks so that, every fall, all the kids were sent back to school with backpacks stuffed with supplies. As a teenager, Martha and her siblings joined a youth center on Hudson Street, where the kids wrote and distributed their own newspaper about Cabrini, since the outside press was so bad.

"Cabrini was a community that held the community together," said Martha. "I don't care what people say."

Neighbors kept an eye on each other and their children. Martha's mother fed not only her own kids—Martha, her seven sisters, and her three brothers—but all the children in her section of their high-rise on Cleveland Street. She used to cook up five or six full boxes of ribs just to feed everyone.

After her mother's death, Martha and little Jajuanna had a two-bedroom apartment all to themselves. There was a washing machine that Martha connected to the kitchen sink faucet because the piping was broken, and a utility closet where Martha strung rope to create a makeshift drying line. Jajuanna had a tiny camping tent that she used to pitch in the middle of her bedroom. The women were insulated from the chaos outside.

Sequestered inside their apartment with their tent and drying laundry, Martha and Jajuanna weren't living the dream, but they were safe. Martha went to college and worked a string of odd jobs that never paid enough to be worth it. Jajuanna played with her *Blue's Clues* stuffed animal dog and grew into a feisty child who was always running around.

The stability was short-lived. In 1999, Biggs was evicted. The one-strike law used to oust Martha Biggs from her home allows housing authorities to evict a family if any of the residents or guests, including the children, are arrested or accused of a crime—whether or not they are later convicted. Like her parents' flight north, Martha's eviction was part of a much broader wave of motion. The following year, Chicago Mayor Richard Daley announced the city's "Plan for Transformation," which called for the eviction of tens of thousands of families living in public housing units that the city had slated for demolition. Over the ensuing decade, Chicago's poor and their public housing towers were "disappeared" from Chicago's skyline. With the one-strike rule as a justification, the housing authority used every possible violation to oust people. Former Cabrini residents said the housing authority even converted the pathways of Cabrini into no-trespassing zones and then planted police officers to pick up the offending pedestrians to speed up evictions.

Housing activist J.R. Fleming inadvertently watched a Hollywood reenactment of these evictions a few months after a wrecking ball tore through the last standing Cabrini tower, known simply as 1230 N. Burling Street. A former Cabrini Green resident and a close friend of Martha, Fleming had come to visit his old neighborhood. Instead, he stumbled into a made-for-TV drama about his and Martha's own life. A television show called *Boss* was filming an episode about public housing demolition in Chicago, exercising Hollywood's unique gift by turning mass displacement into mainstream entertainment.

The majority of Cabrini's remaining three hundred families were gathered around the set watching or were working as extras, acting out an eviction process that might claim them soon. Tension was high; the city had already made it clear that their homes were as disposable as the movie set. More than twenty thousand residents, including Martha and Fleming, had already been evicted from Cabrini Green. The rumor on the block (denied by the city) was that the remaining structures were going to be redeveloped into student housing—a wry comment on the ever expanding University of Chicago campus nearby. Fleming joked with residents about returning to school to get his home back. But when the action started, Fleming fell silent. Slowly, dozens of residents-turned-actors emerged from inside the long beige stretches of row houses, the only structures in Cabrini still standing at the time of the filming. They dragged their feet and carried cardboard boxes, crates and lamps. Their eyes were trained on the asphalt. One man pushed an elderly woman in a wheelchair down the road. Women clasped the hands of young children. It felt like a Great Depression reenactment more than something that could happen throughout the booming Clinton era. After thirty seconds of dejected migration, the director called, "Cut!" Fleming was quiet; as one of the founding members of the Chicago Anti-Eviction Campaign, he'd spent years unsuccessfully trying to fight these types of mass evictions.

"They would never be able to move people this calmly out of Cabrini," he finally said.

In some ways, that was true. Martha wasn't the only one to simply move into another Cabrini apartment after receiving an eviction notice. People forced out of public housing—especially single mothers with children—usually had no place to go; that's why they were in public housing in the first place. One study of Robert Taylor, another public housing development in Chicago, estimated that 25 percent of the residents living there were doing so under the Chicago Housing Authority's radar—either doubled up with family or squatting in one of the many vacant units. According to that estimate, 40 percent of these unauthorized residents were women and children.[59]

But Martha knew that nine women sharing one bathroom couldn't last long. Plus, no one knew when the housing authority would move to evict Martha and her relatives from this apartment, either. Still in her early twenties, Martha found herself charged with finding a place for her and her two daughters to live. She dreamed of finding something—anything—that was safe and stable. But more than that, Martha harbored a bigger dream, one that she carried with her throughout the next decade as she and her children bounced from relatives' homes, empty public housing apartments, vacant houses, shelters, and nights curled in the car. As a young woman whose life was shaped by the forced displacement of her family and tens of thousands of her neighbors in Cabrini, Martha imagined a different way of thinking about housing in the United States—one in which everyone had, at the very at least, a place to put their kids to sleep. The indignities of life as a single mother without a place to live inspired a personal vision that teetered between desperation and utopia, and she developed a mantra: If rats can live for free, we can live for free.

To live as good as rats—it sounds like a bizarre dream, an unthinkable aspiration. But to Martha, it made as much sense as any of the insanity she and her children had endured.

One year after crowding into the two-bedroom apartment in Cabrini, Martha, Jajuanna, and Jimmya moved into a homeless shelter.

THE EXPLOSION

My grandma was born a slave then worked as a nanny. She had five kids, put two through Georgetown and died owning three houses. [Now] I live in a constant state of fear. . . . I am so on the defensive, I sleep with a baseball bat and a machete.

—*Marcella Robinson, North Carolina*

Capitalism never solves its crisis problems. It just moves them around geographically.[60]

—*David Harvey, urban geographer*

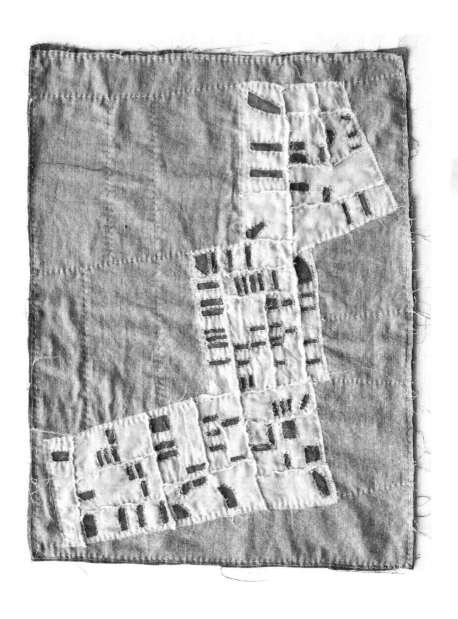

Foreclosure Quilt representing Southern Chase, North Carolina, by Kathryn Clark, 2012. Made from tea-stained voile, cotton, linen, yarn and embroidery thread; 23" x 30". Foreclosures stitched in dark thread.

A TEN-YEAR CRIME SPREE

Griggs Wimbley
Sanford, North Carolina

Griggs spent nine months building his and Audrey's new home on Tempting Church Road. Meanwhile, over in Greensboro, the bank packaged Griggs's loan with hundreds of others and sold the bundle to Chase Manhattan Bank as the First Greensboro Home Equity Loan Trust 1997-1. Three years later, Chase merged with JP Morgan & Co. to become JP Morgan Chase. By then, Griggs's loan was already far gone, packaged once again with other types of debt—credit card loans, student loans, commercial loans, even car loans—into a bundle called a CDO, or collateralized debt obligation, which Chase sold either to private investors or to the government-sponsored Fannie Mae and Freddie Mac. This chain was called the securitization process, because it gave the banks and the mortgage pushers the security of not having to care whether the loan was ever repaid. They'd already cashed out.

After Griggs made the first four payments, First Greensboro hired a company called IMC mortgage services to manage Griggs's payments, which was called "servicing the loan." Griggs grew annoyed because the company was constantly calling him and asking for extra payments or small fees.

"I said, 'Look, I just sent you the money, what the hell is going on?'" he remembers.

Phone harassment by mortgage pushers and servicing companies is fairly common. The Federal Trade Commission reports it receives seventy thousand complaints about debt collectors every year, many of which are mortgage servicing companies.[61] In a personal lawsuit against one lending company, a man in New Hampshire said that employees called both his home and cell phone "almost continuously during the day and evening."[62] One woman in Florida sued her mortgage servicing company, Green Tree Servicing LLC, alleging that the constant harassment—up to nine calls a day, sometimes snidely derisive in tone—killed her husband, who had heart problems and an outstanding balance of less than $700.[63]

Griggs didn't challenge IMC when it demanded minor additional fees.

"I just told them to take it out of my account—300 102 907—that was my checking account. I still know [the numbers] because that's how many times this company called," he said.

One year later, First Greensboro claimed that Griggs had missed his September 1998 payment.[64] He told them he hadn't, and he faxed IMC a copy of the check. Shortly thereafter, he called IMC seeking confirmation that the company had received his proof of September's payment. As he waited on hold, he heard a man's voice in the background say, "I think we got us another one."

Griggs was busy building his first two modular homes on two tracts of land he'd bought across the street, so he didn't think much of those words. He handed the responsibility of paying the mortgage to his wife, Audrey.

Although Audrey didn't understand why, IMC began sending back her checks; first October, then November, and then December. The couple would later learn that it takes three months of missed payments before a mortgage holder can initiate a foreclosure, and that servicing companies rarely accept payments after they believe one has been missed. By the spring, First Greensboro told Audrey that she was delinquent on her loan, but that she could catch up through lump-sum payments of $2,500 to $4,000 a month. Over the next few months, she paid over $10,000.

In July, Griggs was in his backyard clearing the lot with a bulldozer when the sheriff came to deliver foreclosure papers. The eviction was scheduled for August.

"That's how quickly it happened; that's how it all began," said Griggs.

Furious with his wife, Griggs tried to untangle what had happened. The man's whispered words—"we got us another one"—began to haunt him.

"I never forgot," Griggs said more than a decade later. "That's why I'm here now. I wouldn't give up because of what I heard then."

Did IMC plot Griggs's foreclosure—using the company's error in September to push him into default? Did these servicers think they could take advantage of him? Thoughts raced through his head, but time was short. Griggs had less than one month to figure out how to stop the bank from foreclosing on his home. He rushed from lawyer to lawyer without finding anyone who knew how to help. Finally, he saw an ad in the paper for an attorney who claimed he could save Griggs's home. The man convinced Griggs to declare Chapter 13 bankruptcy, which would stay the foreclosure and allow Griggs time to make the unpaid payments, known as the arrears. Griggs was reluctant. He explained that he wasn't bankrupt; he was making $80,000 a year. Plus, he was ahead on his mortgage after his wife's lump-sum payments, not behind. But he was out of time and options. Griggs declared Chapter 13 bankruptcy.

"I used to wake up in a cold sweat, thinking: I'm not supposed to be in Chapter 13," he said.

His loan servicer switched to another small company called CALMCO, which later renamed itself Greenwich Capital and Olympus Servicing and then quickly disappeared. Within less than a year, Griggs's servicer changed again, this time to Fairbanks Capital Holding Corp. To his disbelief, Griggs was supposedly behind on his payments, again.

Fairbanks embodied everything that was sleazy, greedy, and flat-out fraudulent about mortgage servicing companies. By 2002, the company was the biggest servicer of predatory mortgages in the United States, managing more than 500,000 loans worth $50 billion. Predatory mortgage bankers targeted and ensnared people with below-average credit scores, charging higher interest rates and other fees because they were extending loans to "riskier" individuals. In reality, the lenders—not the borrowers—posed the real risks. Because of the securitization process, the lending companies had no incentive to design loans that would actually be paid back, since they would immediately be packaged and sold on Wall Street, as had happened to Griggs's loan.

Predatory mortgage pushing exploded in the late 1990s and early 2000s after decades of lending and banking deregulation. By 2005 and 2006, 20 percent of all loans initiated were predatory. Most relied on ballooning payments (these were called adjustable-rate mortgages), which were legalized after the passage of the Garn-St. Germain Depository Institutions Act of 1982. The interest rates on these mortgages would be low for the first few years, and then skyrocket to up to 20 percent of the loan's value. The most predatory loan Wall Street concocted was called "an interest-only, negative-amortizing, adjustable-rate loan," an absolutely incomprehensible way of saying that the total amount owed actually *increased* as time went on.

In the film *Inside Job*, consumer advocate Robert Gnaizda

recounts showing Federal Reserve chairman Alan Greenspan 150 examples of complex, adjustable-rate mortgages.

"If you had a doctorate in math, you wouldn't be able to understand which of these was good for you, and which wasn't," Gnaizda remembers Greenspan telling him.[65]

Borrowers have been wickedly criticized as being both ignorant and indulgent for signing on to predatory loans that they wouldn't be able to pay back. But the mortgage pushers not only wrote the loans to be incomprehensible, they often outright lied about the terms of the agreement. According to the Federal Trade Commission, one company sold "15-year balloon loans," in which, after fifteen years, "the consumer will owe a large lump sum payment that is usually greater than 80 percent of the loan principal." Since that was not a loan that most people would agree to, the company simply chose to lie at the time of the sale—both in writing and in conversation—by "representing that the loan does not contain a balloon payment."[66] In the late 1990s and early 2000s, the Federal Trade Commission sued dozens of mortgage pushing companies for similar cases of deception: lying about the loan's terms, tacking on charges that the mortgage holder had not agreed to, and even, in one case, foreclosing on people who were current on their payments.[67]

Griggs's loan had a high interest rate—nearly 12 percent—but it was a flat-rate loan, and he thought he would be able to afford the payments with his income. His problem was not the predatory mortgage industry but the even more fraud-ridden servicing companies hired by the banks to receive mortgage payments.

"See this little charge right here," Griggs said, pointing at one of his Fairbanks statements. The bill listed $6.48 owed for something called "interest on advance for the month," another $10 for "broker price options," and a handful of other minor charges, including a "history fee." Within a few years, the Federal Trade Commission would declare all these charges illegal.

"This little charge here, no one would notice it," he continued. "But $6.50 times 350,000 homeowners"—he pulled out his calculator—"well, that's $22 million."

As Griggs was trying to make sense of the fees, the Federal Trade Commission was investigating Fairbanks for defrauding hundreds of thousands of people, Griggs included.

One of Fairbanks's favorite tricks, according to the Federal Trade Commission's complaint, was to delay posting a monthly payment, only to turn around and charge a never-ending cycle of late fees. For Griggs, this deception wasn't just an economic inconvenience; it was destroying his life. In 2002, Fairbanks began hounding him for a missing $680. He sent a check; it wasn't posted. He drove up to Durham to pay in person, only to be told he was current on his bill. A few weeks later, Fairbanks once again demanded the money, saying his fees had finally been processed. Griggs sent a check, but he'd already been dismissed from Chapter 13 for failure to stay current on his bills.

"It bothered me pretty bad," Griggs said, his face bunching up with contained emotion. By now, Griggs knew his credit was shot; he worried he'd never be able to buy those one hundred acres of land.

He re-filed for Chapter 13 bankruptcy, only to learn that his arrears had *increased* rather than decreased since the first filing. Somehow Griggs owed even more than when he'd first declared bankruptcy, which made no sense to him, since he'd been following the payment plan laid out by the court. Reviewers ordered by the federal government to analyze the banks' paperwork would later reveal that mortgage-pushing companies frequently levied exorbitant illegal charges against families in Chapter 13, which often landed families in foreclosure the moment bankruptcy ended. One reviewer said that every single bankruptcy case he examined included the banks perpetrating some form of fraud.[68] But Griggs couldn't convince the bankruptcy court that the charges he was accused of didn't add up. The lawyers, his bankruptcy trustee, and even the judge seemed to be biased toward Fairbanks and Greensboro—even outright complicit in the deception. After one hearing, he watched the judge and all the lawyers, including his own, exit the courtroom laughing.

"Most people would have given up, quit," he said. "I've even cried. These people . . . the judge laughed at me. They were working for the banks to take my money and steal our homes." He paused. "It really bothered me. You're going to make me. . . ." He trailed off, then resumed. "I had a home modular dealership, and they caught me up in all this stuff."

Griggs's health worsened. His knees were aching from the years of construction work, and the stress of being in Chapter 13 had elevated his blood pressure. He was on various medications to control it, but he still experienced moments of dizziness and lightheadedness, especially when driving back and forth from the bankruptcy hearings. But the worst part was the emotional effects: Griggs felt increasing angry and alone. The continuing foreclosure process hadn't only threatened his house; it was eating away at his dreams.

In 2003, Fairbanks settled with the Federal Trade Commission on allegations of fraud, and the company shelled out $40 million in consumer refunds.

The government celebrated.

"Today's settlement makes clear that HUD and the FTC

are serious about protecting consumers from those who would try to steal their American Dream," declared Mel Martinez, the Secretary for Housing and Urban Development (HUD).[69]

But instead of a reimbursement, Griggs received another foreclosure notice. By March 2004, Griggs found himself back in housing court. He arrived armed with information from the settlement, forcing Fairbanks's lawyer to drop the foreclosure. But the ordeal wasn't over. The company changed its name to Select Portfolio Services and remained Griggs's servicer. Like the majority of mortgage-pushing and -servicing companies that have settled with the Federal Trade Commission since 1998, it was allowed to remain in business both during and after the investigation.

As Griggs began to research the companies with which he was dealing, the inside of his home began overflowing with evidence of the mortgage company's wrongdoings. File cabinets and cardboard boxes sprouted in his office, basement, and bedroom, which he quickly stuffed with court transcripts, FTC complaints, SEC reports, news articles, legal manuals, and a seemingly endless stack of foreclosure filings against him. As the years went on, his stacks upon stacks of papers grew into a paper trail of what he called "a ten-year crime spree." Taken together, it was a testimony—a museum exhibit, almost—to the unraveling of his dreams and those of millions of others.

"I've got piles—thousands of papers. I can show you some cheating," he said, picking through the dozens of filing boxes and loose stacks of court documents, news articles, bank statements, attorney payments, and letters to the Attorney General and President Obama. In his office were stacks of reports like the hundred-page Federal Reserve document "Understanding the Securitization of Subprime Mortgage Credit." In the basement were piles of books, such as *Represent Yourself in Court*, and a whole shelf of binders with neat, handwritten labels: "Fairbanks Lawsuit," "Foreclosure Filings," "FBI." He hired assistants to come in and help him organize the evidence, but he was so particular and protective of the paper trail that he always ended up asking them to leave.

In July 2006, GMAC mortgage claimed that it was now servicing Griggs's loan. He was off in Chapter 13, but his problems were far from over. Like Fairbanks, GMAC was secretly engaging in a host of illegal activities that would soon place the company at the center of a massive scandal in the mortgage industry and keep Griggs's home perpetually in foreclosure.

Within the first few months of assuming the loan, GMAC signed a foreclosure affidavit for Griggs's house, even though he had paid the company consistently.

"Here I am, I'm sending you my money, and they say, 'Welcome to GMAC. We're putting your house in foreclosure,'" Griggs said.

It felt as if GMAC hadn't even read his loan history before authorizing the foreclosure, which was probably true. Four years later, a GMAC mortgage employee testified in a disposition that he and his team had signed "a round number of ten thousand" foreclosure affidavits every week without actually reading the documents or verifying the information.[70] This admission kicked off an investigation into the practice, which later became known as robo-signing.

"All the banks are the same, GMAC is the only one who's gotten caught," a Florida-based lawyer told Bloomberg News as the controversy unfolded in the fall of 2010. "This could be huge."[71]

Within one year, investigations revealed that Bank of America, JP Morgan Chase, Citi Bank, HSBC, Wells Fargo, US Bank,

Deutsche Bank, Litton Loan Servicing (a mortgage servicer owned by Goldman Sachs), and others were all engaging in similar practices: authorizing hundreds of thousands of foreclosure filings every month without ever checking if the people—like Griggs—were actually current. One robo-signer named Chris Pindley signed not his own name but the name "Linda Green" because it was shorter, and he was pressured to sign four thousand foreclosure affidavits every day.[72] Other employees notarized the documents, testifying that the signatories were who they said they were and had done what they said they'd done, even though they knew otherwise.

A HUD investigation later revealed that robo-signing of affidavits often led to foreclosures based on incomplete or inaccurate information. In one study, HUD reviewed thirty-six foreclosures at JP Morgan Chase—the bank that owned Griggs's mortgage—and revealed that in only *one* of the thirty-six cases did the bank have documentation proving even the most basic information: what the family supposedly owed on the mortgage.[73]

Throughout 2006, Griggs trudged back and forth from one foreclosure hearing to the next. GMAC's robo-signing practices had not yet been revealed, and he was constantly at risk of losing his house. In one month—July 2006—he succeeded in getting one foreclosure dismissed, only to receive a new foreclosure filing two days later. Griggs believed that much of the confusion in his paperwork was caused by his previous servicer, Select Portfolio Services (SPS). Between 2003 and 2006, SPS had continued to plague Griggs with even more of the illegal fees and penalties that it had inflicted upon him under the name Fairbanks.

Griggs wrote to the North Carolina Office of the Commissioner of Banks, an agency that was supposed to oversee banking and lending regulation and investigate cases of fraud, to inform the office about SPS's abuse. At the time, the commissioner was a lawyer named Joseph A. Smith, who, before his appointment in 2002, had worked as the senior vice president and general counsel to RBC Centura, which later became PNC Bank. Griggs waited years for a reply. Finally, in 2009, Smith's office wrote to Griggs saying that there had been no problems whatsoever with his loan— neither with its origination nor with its servicing. Suspicious, Griggs began to investigate Smith himself, learning that when he had served as vice president at RBC Centura, the bank owned 49 percent of First Greensboro Home Equity, the very company responsible for originating Griggs's loan. No wonder, then, that Smith had outright dismissed any allegations of fraud that had to do with his own business record.

"I wrote the Governor telling her who she had hired, what he had been doing before working for the state," said Griggs. To him, the revolving door between the banking industry and the very agencies charged with regulating that industry looked a whole lot like government collusion.

The Wall-Street-to-Washington pipeline is nothing new. The very first chairman of the Securities and Exchange Commission, which was created after the Great Depression as "the main overseer and regulator of the U.S. securities market," was himself the former president of the Columbia Trust Bank.[74] Yet the revolving door has been spinning ever more quickly in the last two decades. The CEO of Goldman Sachs, for example, seems to have a guaranteed position as the future Secretary of the Treasury, a cabinet position that was filled by Goldman leaders under Presidents Clinton, George W. Bush, and Obama. One of JP Morgan's managing directors became a senior official in Clinton's Treasury Department; the chief Goldman Sachs lobbyist became the chief of staff in the Treasury Department under Obama.

The Federal Reserve has also been filled with former Goldman men, including the company's chief economist (later the president of the New York Federal Reserve) and its chairman (who kept his same title at the Fed). Another senior official at Goldman became the head of the Commodity Futures Trading Commission. The list goes on and on.[75]

With the government's regulatory agencies crawling with former and future bankers, whistleblowers like Griggs find these men more often ignoring widespread fraud than actually fulfilling their jobs. But Griggs wasn't going to accept what he saw as a criminal collusion between the North Carolina Office of the Commission of the Banks and his original mortgage company, First Greensboro. He wrote furious, certified-mail letters to the governor, the Federal Trade Commission, and the President, asking for help and warning them about what was going on. In these letters, he explained that he'd uncovered filing cabinets' worth of deception. In addition to Smith's conflict of interest, First Greensboro seemed to be at the center of shady activity, which included tampering with court transcripts and deleting the online records of bankruptcy cases of people who had First Greensboro Home Equity loans.

But Griggs was worried about more than just First Greensboro or even North Carolina. By the beginning of 2006, at the height of the housing bubble, Griggs was worried about the entire United States economy. The more he learned, the more he thought that the frenzied increase in speculative trading—betting on what would happen in the future—was dangerous and absurd.

"If you got a pair of boots," he said, gesturing toward his feet as he began to explain speculative trading, also called derivatives,

"I can put options on the shoestrings that they'll stay tied up, and then I can bet that if you go through the briars, they'll come unloose. And then we can have a bet on whether the briars will pull the shoes loose or whether they will not. Anything you can think of you can bet on Wall Street. That's what it's all about."

By 2000, derivatives constituted an unregulated $50 trillion market. Between speculative trading and the increase in predatory mortgages, the price of houses grew higher and higher, doubling between 1996 and 2006. This overinflation of house values was called a bubble—and many considered it the biggest in United States history.

The fact that everyone (besides the families in the homes) could take out insurance on these loans fueled the dizzying increase in predatory mortgages. Through the securitization process, the mortgage-pushing companies and Wall Street banks quickly profited from the loans and then sold them off to investors through collateralized debt obligations. These investors, meanwhile, bought insurance on the CDOs so that they were protected from any losses in case the financial products failed. AIG, the world's largest insurance company at the time, issued $500 billion worth of insurance on loans during the housing bubble. Other speculators who had no relationship with the CDOs could still bet against them (and turn a profit if they failed) by buying credit default swaps (CDSs) from AIG as well.

In other words, the banks and investors could engineer their bets so that they got paid whether the briars pulled out those shoestrings or not.

Griggs wrote a sixteen-page letter to Lynne Weaver, the assistant attorney general of North Carolina, warning her of an impending wave of foreclosures nearly one year before the housing market collapsed.

"All of these servicing companies including First Greensboro [are] owned by JP Morgan, Chase Manhattan bank. These loans are put into packages and sold on Wall Street. The servicing companies are robbing and stealing homes for profit. No one is seeing what is happening in the background. . . . I am, I feel, a rather intelligent individual and have had no help in getting my case in court," he added.

But Griggs was the type of whistleblower who never got his day of glory. Weaver didn't even reply until two years later, well after Bear Stearns failed, then Lehman Brothers, then AIG, then Fannie Mae and Freddie Mac. By the time she replied in 2009, the national unemployment rate was 10 percent, and the banks had already evicted families from nearly two million repossessed homes.

Griggs's physical and mental health further deteriorated. Still bitter from those few months where Audrey assumed responsibility for the loan, he thought about leaving his wife. His knees were shot; he needed surgery. But worst of all, his anger and sense of alienation threatened to consume him. With a fierceness in keeping with his stormy personality, Griggs returned to God after years of absence from the Tempting Congregation.

Bolstered by his faith, Griggs filed a lawsuit in North Carolina District Court against Select Portfolio Services for violating the 2003 Federal Trade Commission injunction. Fed up with lawyers, Griggs wrote both the original and the amended complaint himself, which the judge later criticized as being "disorganized, rambling, and at times incoherent." But the quality of the complaint didn't matter. In July 2009, the judge dismissed the case because the "FTC Act does not create a private right of action for enforcement of the FTC Act."[76] In other words, everyday people don't have the right to sue companies that have broken the rules established by the Federal Trade Commission's settlement.

That same year, Griggs watched as President Obama gave $9.9 billion to six mortgage-pushing companies to "help struggling homeowners," one of the companies being Select Services Portfolio. In 2012, Griggs again watched, indignant, as Smith resigned from his post as commissioner so that he could take on a bigger and better responsibility: overseeing the allocation of the $26 billion settlement the government had reached with the banks over robo-signing and other criminal acts of fraud. Part of that settlement required the banks to hire consultants to review the paperwork of nearly four million completed foreclosures to better understand the industry's crimes. Instead, in January 2013, the banks once again settled with government—this time for $8.5 billion—in order to hastily stop the foreclosure reviews and, as one *New York Times* columnist wrote, "push those misdeeds under a $8.5 billion rug."[77]

Over the course of a decade, Griggs received an estimated forty foreclosure filings since the first one in 1999, all of which he fought relentlessly in court. Finally, the assistant clerk of court for Lee County promised Griggs that he wouldn't have to worry about eviction any longer. In North Carolina, the county clerk's office must sign the writ to initiate eviction before the sheriff's office will take action.

But keeping the house was a small consolation to Griggs. The fraudulent foreclosures had destroyed his plans to build one hundred acres of homes. He felt as if he'd lost not only his career and his credit but also his whole life—and no one even understood.

"Imagine seeing this here happen, witnessing it, and thinking you're all alone," said Griggs. "It's like someone stealing your identity," he said.

He no longer thought that he'd been the victim of a mistake or a single instance of fraud. Instead, he saw the last ten years of his life as an illuminating and devastating picture of how the U.S. economic system actually worked when in its normal state. What had first appeared to be an isolated incident of crime and deception now seemed to have enveloped the entire country. It wasn't just that he had been a victim of corruption; it was that he was living in a corrupt society.

Griggs became depressed, angry, and even apocalyptic about the country's future.

"The world is going to blow up; it's going to catch on fire. I've seen nothing but cheating," he said.

Gone was the entrepreneurial and hopeful Griggs Wimbley who so believed in the American Dream that he aspired to build houses. That identity had been stolen from him, and in its place there emerged a man who believed there was a deep sickness within the nation. Little did he know as he sat in his foreclosed home in rural North Carolina how many other people felt the same way.

LORD, I AM SINKING

Bertha Garrett
Detroit, Michigan

In far Northwest Detroit, Bertha and William Garrett paid off their first mortgage—a $40,000 loan—in full. In 1998, they took out a second mortgage for $45,000 from a company called Conti Mortgage and Lender.

"They told me that I needed to invest in the equity of my home, and that an adjustable-rate mortgage would set me up for investments," said Bertha. It was a common ploy that mortgage pushers used in the late 1990s: Call up someone—often an older woman—who wouldn't necessarily take out a loan and tell her all about how her money was just sitting there, wasting away, when it could be used to better her family's future. Bertha and William had children in college and ministry school, and an extra year's worth of tuition sounded like a good idea.

Bertha agreed to the loan, which Conti quickly resold to Bank of New York Mellon. But instead of setting Bertha up to make smart investments, the predatory loan plunged her into debt as $45,000 ballooned to a staggering $190,000.

Predatory mortgages existed long before the late 1990s and early 2000s. In the 1950s and 1960s, they were common in the redlined urban neighborhoods where major banks and the federal government refused to extend loans, opening a secondary market for exploitive mortgage pushers, then called loan sharks. After decades of organizing, including massive mortgage loan strikes in Chicago, Congress passed the Fair Housing Act of 1968 and the Community Reinvestment Act of 1977, which ended redlining and essentially destroyed the loan sharks' market.

But predatory mortgages didn't disappear. Instead, as Reagan deregulated the savings and loan industry in the 1980s, and Clinton deregulated the banking industry in the 1990s, predatory mortgage pushers were no longer confined to minority neighborhoods where there was no oversight or access to federal funds. Instead, mortgage pushers began targeting whites as well as people of color. As a team of housing scholars wrote in *American Quarterly*, "The predatory exploitation of the urban core has gone mainstream."[78]

But even though financial exploitation had become more widespread nationally, predatory mortgage pushers still primarily targeted African Americans and Latinos. According to the Center for Responsible Lending:

> Loan type and race and ethnicity are strongly linked. African Americans and Latinos were much more likely to receive high interest rate (subprime) loans and loans with features that are associated with higher foreclosures, specifically prepayment penalties and hybrid or option ARMs [adjustable-rate mortgages]. These disparities were evident even comparing borrowers within the same credit score ranges. In fact, the disparities were especially pronounced for borrowers with higher credit scores. For example, among borrowers with a FICO score of over 660 (indicating good credit), African Americans and Latinos received a high interest rate loan more than three times as often as white borrowers.[79]

The Center for Responsible Lending called this disparity a "dual mortgage market," in which families of color had to navigate mortgage pushers' predatory track, while white families were offered conventional mortgages. The racial difference in who was allowed to buy what type of mortgage was so stark that the word "subprime" (the industry's term for predatory loans) became "a demographic category as much as a financial definition."[80]

Affidavits by two of Wells Fargo's most successful mortgage sellers reveal just how aggressively the industry targeted African Americans specifically for these predatory mortgages. In sworn testimonies in 2009, Elizabeth Jacobson and Tony Pascal, who both worked in Wells Fargo's Baltimore branch, explained the myriad ways the company institutionalized racist practices. According to Pascal, the predatory lending division intentionally sent out promotional material to the city's zip codes with the highest percentage of African American residents. These packets, Pascal explained, could be printed in multiple so-called languages, one of which was "African American." (He brought with him to court a computer screenshot proving that the company's computer system offered this language option, perhaps anticipating disbelief.)

Jacobson explained that the company specifically targeted African American churches for predatory loans, and that it went out of its way to make sure African Americans were the face of the company in these settings. Jacobson, who is white, was barred from giving presentations to African American congregations, instead hiring an African American saleswoman to focus exclusively on selling these toxic products to the churches. Loan sellers never, meanwhile, gave presentations aimed at selling predatory loans to white congregations.

"Subprime loan officers did not market or target white churches for subprime loans," she testified. "When it came to marketing, any reference to 'church' or 'churches' was understood as code for African-American or black churches."[81]

Wells Fargo and all other major mortgage pushing companies financially incentivized loan salesmen to steer people into predatory mortgages. According to the U.S. Department of Justice, the nation's largest mortgage companies used a two-tier system to guide a borrower towards a mortgage loan. Here's how it worked. First, the company used algorithms to calculate what loan a person qualified for based on his or her credit scores. The better the person's credit rating, the lower the interest rate and the smaller the fees. The system compiled these interest rates and fees into a rate sheet, which was sent to the loan salesman but not shown to the borrower. Here's where it got tricky. The salesman was allowed to change the terms of the loans (such as raising the interest rate or tacking on fees), and he got paid more if he was able to charge the borrower above the rate sheet's price.[82]

This pay structure incentivized loan salesmen to trick their African American customers into riskier and more expensive loans—even if they qualified for a "prime" mortgage.

As Pascal explained:

> Because Wells Fargo made a higher profit on subprime loans, the company put "bounties" on minority borrowers. By this I mean that loan officers received cash incentives to aggressively market subprime loans in minority communities. If a loan officer referred a borrower who should have qualified for a prime loan to a subprime loan, the loan officer would receive a bonus. Loan officers were able to do this because they had the discretion to decide which loan products to offer and to determine the interest rate and fees charged to the borrower. Since loan officers

made more money when they charged higher interest rates
and fees to borrowers, there was a great financial incentive to
put as many minority borrowers as possible into subprime
loans and to charge these borrowers higher rates and fees.

These types of perverse financial incentives—such as placing a
"bounty" on African American lenders—created a racist internal
culture. Pascal testified that he often heard other predatory loan
salesmen "mimic and make fun of their minority customers by
using racial slurs. They referred to subprime loans made in minority
communities as 'ghetto loans.'" As for the customers themselves,
Pascal's colleagues called them "mud people," while his branch
manager openly called them "niggers."[83]

In the *California Law Review*, scholar Benjamin Howell explains
how predatory lending perpetrated by the largest Wall Street
banks during the 1990s and 2000s took advantage of the history of
housing discrimination, targeting redlined neighborhoods because
they knew the demand for mortgages was high.

"Where lending discrimination once took a binary form—
bigoted loan officers rejecting loan applicants because of their skin
color—the new model of discrimination is exploitation," writes
Howell. "Unscrupulous lenders now prey on a history of racial
redlining by aggressively marketing overpriced loan products with
onerous terms in the same neighborhoods where mainstream
lenders once refused to lend."[84]

Since 2008, three of the nation's largest banks—Bank of
America, Wells Fargo, and SunTrust Bank—have settled with
the U.S. Department of Justice on charges of widespread and
institutional lending discrimination.

But as Bertha watched her mortgage payments balloon in the

early 2000s, she didn't know anything about discrimination and predatory lending. All she knew was that her debt was spiraling out of control. Bertha and William turned to their daughter, Michelle, for help. In 2003, she and her husband bought the house from her parents and negotiated the total debt down to $125,000. Briefly, their monthly payments were only $900, but they soon increased to $1,100, then $1,300.

Money wasn't, however, the biggest challenge in Bertha's life. William had fallen ill, and he suffered a series of strokes. After the first, brain hemorrhaging left him frequently disoriented, and he began wandering around the neighborhood like a lost child. Later, after his second stroke and cataract surgery, he was rendered legally blind. Bertha was grateful to live on a close-knit block; her neighbors promised to keep an eye on William when he ventured outside.

William could barely see any longer, so he closed his barbershop, cutting off his and Bertha's only source of income. Bertha applied for a loan modification, hoping that this one would decrease the payments. Instead, they rose to $1,650 a month. The two families split the monthly payments, Bertha and William selling land and furniture to scrape together $1,000 a month, and Michelle and her husband covering the rest, in addition to their own mortgage payments.

But that arrangement didn't last long. One night as Michelle watched the evening news, she learned that the restaurant franchise where she worked had gone out of business. She had been laid off—and no one even bothered to tell her. Some of her co-workers who hadn't caught the news segment arrived for work only to find the doors locked. The mortgage payments jumped to $2,500 a month. The bank kept selling the mortgage note from one servicer to the next; Bertha could barely keep up with where she should send the checks. For five months, the two families scraped together $2,500. Then, finally, they could no longer pay.

"Lord, I am sinking," Bertha scrawled in tight handwriting in one of her many notebooks filled with poems and gospel songs.

"My husband is blind, we are without money and have no way to pay."

Just before Christmas in 2010, Bertha found a notice of foreclosure posted on her front door.

For many families, realizing that their home may no longer be theirs is the worst moment of their lives.

Monique White, a mother in North Minneapolis, recalls learning that her home had been sold in an auction without U.S. Bank, the owner of her mortgage, even telling her.

"I went to turn on the heat and my furnace wasn't working," she said. "I called the company to come out and check the gas, but they said they couldn't, because I wasn't the homeowner. . . . I was devastated . . . I was just bawling." It was the middle of January and White had young children, so she turned on the oven to heat her home as she tried to figure out what to do.

The shame of foreclosure is so great, sometimes the fact that people will know about it seems worse than losing the house itself.

"I didn't even want my family to know," remembers Connie Freeman, another Minneapolis resident. When her husband, Mark, attended a union rally protesting foreclosures and one of his colleagues convinced him to speak, Connie was devastated that a whole crowd of people now knew their secret.

"I was almost hysterical," she said.

This silence reinforces the sense of isolation, but breaking the silence is not easy. In a nation where private property and legal contracts have become valued more than anything, the idea of default is terrifying.

Steve and Pamela Douglass, a couple in rural Minnesota, remember the moment they realized that they couldn't pay both their mortgage and their medical bills.

"In 2010 I went to HUD [for help] and filled out all the paperwork," Pamela Douglass said. "And that just made me sick because I realized that I didn't have anywhere near enough money to pay these bills."

Their lawyer advised them to default on their mortgage, but when the end of the month arrived, the two were frantic.

"We were just bawling and fighting and screaming at each other because we do *not* not pay our bills," said Douglass.

Others are not able to endure these feelings of shame and desperation. There are no national statistics, but the rising trend of foreclosure-related suicides is obvious from the horror stories plastered across the front page of local newspapers. In Taunton, Massachusetts, a woman named Carlene Balderrama awoke on the morning of her home's foreclosure in July 2008, faxed her last note to her mortgage lender, PHH Mortgage Corp., and then shot herself with her husband's rifle. The note read: "By the time you foreclose on my house, I'll be dead."[85] In March 2012, a man shot himself and another woman hanged herself after their Philadelphia homes were foreclosed on and sold at sheriff's sales. The woman, Lynda Clark, lived alone on Philadelphia's South Side, and her hanging body was discovered by the sheriff deputies tasked with posting the eviction notice on her door.[86] A ninety-year-old woman in Akron, Ohio, shot herself in the chest in October 2008 when the police arrived at the door of the home she had lived in for thirty-eight years.[87]

Like foreclosures themselves, these suicides are creeping into tiny towns and bustling cities in all corners of the country.

Homeowners have either shot themselves or burned to death, often with family members, in puritanical Stamford, Connecticut (settled in 1641); pastoral Ocala, Florida (1:7 horse to human ratio countywide[88]); stately Roswell, Georgia (manufacturer of the Confederate soldiers'"Roswell gray"uniforms); booming Houston, Texas (home of the world's largest livestock show and rodeo); and various cities across the Golden State of California (Los Angeles, Newbury Park, and Santee, to name just a few).[89] According to one count, foreclosure and other devastations wrought by the economic crisis have caused more than two hundred people to kill themselves, and sometimes their family members, since 2008.[90] As journalist Nick Turse wrote that same year, "Wall Street's financial meltdown is beginning to be measured not only in dollars and cents, but also in blood. Without debt- or mortgage-forgiveness, more casualties are sure to come."[91]

This suicidal feeling of shame is one of the financial industry's most powerful products, backed by centuries of literature, art, architecture, sermons, advertisements, and propaganda that have advanced the social doctrine that a home demonstrates not only a family's economic worth and class position, but also its moral value. This ideology reinforces the twisted view that well-painted shutters and white picket fences signify a winner's dedication and hard work, and a foreclosure sign denotes a loser's failure.

The argument is particularly dangerous considering the racism embedded in predatory home mortgages. Given the well-documented discrimination, is viewing foreclosure as a mark of poor character that far from the more overt bigotry of seeing race as the indicator of inferiority? Perhaps it's closer than most would like to admit, but the symbolism of foreclosure is one that few take the time to fully analyze—until they have to.

Like so many others, Bertha kept the foreclosure a secret from almost everyone in her life. She couldn't tell her husband. His health was worsening; he was cycling in and out of the hospital. When he was home, he would sometimes trip and fall. Other times he would wander around the neighborhood.

"My fear was that I would lose my husband. I saw him standing outside one day, and I thought to myself: They would have to drag him out of here," said Bertha. "I couldn't tell my husband we wouldn't have Thanksgiving in the house and that we could be evicted." After so much of her life had been devoted to making a safe home for William and their children, she couldn't imagine not protecting him now.

Bertha's baby girl, Alisha, was another person Bertha kept from knowing about the foreclosure. The girl wanted to be just like her older siblings, whose backyard weddings she'd attended when she was young.

"Momma, I want to get married in this yard," she often told her mother.

Bertha felt paralyzed.

"I just rocked in the chair, and I wanted to scream," she remembers.

The Garretts were far from the only family in their neighborhood whose house was in jeopardy. Bertha's next-door neighbor was also is foreclosure. Bertha didn't know, even though she visited the bedridden woman a few times a week to deliver cooked dinners. The family across the street was in foreclosure, too.

In fact, the landscape of this entire Detroit neighborhood was quietly turning to patchwork as the banks forced family after family out of their homes.

"Five years ago, people were in all these houses," said Mike Shane, an organizer with Moratorium Now! who lives only a few streets away from Bertha's home. "Now it's a completely different area. It's just been wiped out," he said.

Between 2000 and 2010, Detroit lost a quarter of a million residents. This exodus encompassed a full 25 percent of the city's population, the largest percentage loss in the city's history. Detroit's population has been declining since the 1950s, when it was the fourth-largest city in the United States. But this last decade's wave of depopulation was entirely different, because it wasn't voluntary.

Through a foreclosure process tainted with racism, banks forced—and continue to force—hundreds of thousands of people out of Detroit, many of whom, like the Garretts, wanted to stay. As housing lawyer Jerry Goldberg writes, "Not one of the many newspaper articles discussing this lost population puts the blame where it belongs—on the major banks, which have leveled neighborhoods throughout Detroit with mass foreclosures driven by racist, predatory lending."[92]

From 2000 to 2012, banks foreclosed on more than a hundred thousand homes in Detroit.[93] At times, the rate of eviction was so high that the city hired additional contract workers—whom residents dubbed "Blackwater bailiffs"—to keep pace. One of the main causes of foreclosure was the extremely high number of predatory mortgages in this majority African American city. Between 2004 and 2006, 73 percent of the new mortgages in the city were predatory loans, compared to about 20 percent nationally.[94]

Perhaps nothing proves the forced nature of this exodus out of Detroit better than the handful of desperate people who have brandished weapons in standoffs with the eviction bailiffs. Only a few blocks from Bertha's house, an armed man barricaded himself in his house in 2012 in a futile attempt to stop his eviction. A few years earlier, a man in the Detroit suburb of Allen Park was shot and killed by a SWAT team when he tried to defend his home from being repossessed. Bertha was a peaceful woman, but she understood the collective feeling of desperation.

"We are fighting for a city that so many have already declared abandoned," Bertha said.

In executing a forced repopulation of a quarter of Detroit's residents, profit-obsessed bankers are quietly waging an economic war against the government of Detroit and its people. The rumors about $1 houses may be exaggerated, but the sharp decline in home prices combined with ballooning mortgage principals have indeed created a Kafkaesque financial market. Down the street from the Garretts, a house sold outright for $3,500 while Bertha was making $2,500 mortgage payments every month. Across the street, a neighbor owed $140,000 on a house that was appraised at $9,800—almost fifteen times less than what he owed. The authority of Wall Street and the financial markets crumbled as families realized that they somehow owed up to *twenty* times what their homes were worth.

Property devaluations occur because each additional foreclosure drags down the value of surrounding homes, pushing the neighbors further underwater on their mortgages and increasing the likelihood that they, too, will default. Even the International Monetary Fund, an organization best known for its dogmatic adherence to "free-market" capitalism, admits the danger of these property value spirals on the surrounding community's economy.

"The associated negative price effects in turn reduce economic activity through a number of self-reinforcing contractionary spirals," the report stated. "Such externalities—banks and households ignoring the social cost of defaults and fire sales—may justify policy intervention aimed at stopping household defaults, foreclosures, and fire sales."[95]

When property values and the number of residents plummet, the effect is a massive erosion of the tax base. Every single foreclosure costs the government approximately $2,000 in lost property tax revenue, according to an analysis of foreclosures in California.[96] Additionally, local city governments are forced to carry out the evictions and absorb other foreclosure-related costs, which average just over $19,000 per house.[97] Foreclosures in the Detroit metro area, therefore, have cost the local government $220 million in lost property tax revenue and as much as $2 billion in government-absorbed foreclosure costs.[98]

These types of bank-imposed debts have pushed Detroit's local government to the brink of collapse, making it nearly impossible for the city to fund even the most necessary services like public schools and police and fire departments. Throughout 2012 and 2013, the budget crisis was so acute that the state repeatedly threatened to take over the city's operations and finances through Michigan's emergency financial manager law. Finally, on March 1, 2013, Michigan Governor Rick Snyder announced the largest state takeover of a U.S. city in the nation's history, appointing a single man, Kevyn D. Orr, to take control of the entire city government of Detroit. As the *New York Times* wrote, "the emergency-manager law gives Mr. Orr extraordinary powers to reshape the city," including the right to sell off parts of the city, break union contracts and fire local elected officials.[99]

The imposition of the emergency manager sparked protests and outcry across Detroit, particularly given the increasingly racialized use of takeovers across the state. After Detroit's takeover, six mostly black cities were being controlled by emergency managers, meaning that nearly half of all African Americans living in Michigan were under the jurisdiction of unelected officials.

"It is the civil rights issue of our time," Reverend Wendell

Anthony, pastor of the Fellowship Chapel in Detroit, told *The Washington Post*. "I didn't vote for an emergency manager. I voted for a mayor. I did not give up my right to vote on the whims and fancies of a law that we believe is unconstitutional and immoral... We view it as another step in the direction of voter suppression and vote oppression."[100]

Reverend David Bullock, pastor of the Greater St. Matthew Baptist Church, explained that the implications of Michigan's emergency manager law go far beyond the temporary issue of local city council meetings. It's about using the city's financial insecurity to impose a form of martial economics—one that could easily be replicated in cities and towns across the country.

"The real security question for rich people is financial security," he said. "It's no longer '68 and '69—the hot riot summers. They are no longer worried about physical security. They are worried about their money."

When it comes to Wall Street, Bullock is right. Despite the emergency manager's nearly unrivaled power, there is one contract that Orr can't break: Detroit's annual $600 million interest payments to Wall Street banks.

The city's landscape is testimony to the systemic effects of mass eviction and the defunding—and resulting disenfranchisement—of local government. On the East Side of the city, entire square miles are fully vacant except for the occasional deer or fox scampering through the shells of old industrial plants. Overhead, lazy blimps advertise scrap metal to no one. One sign, erected on Eight Mile Road, reads: WARNING! THIS CITY IS INFESTED BY CRACKHEADS. SECURE YOUR BELONGINGS AND PRAY FOR YOUR LIFE. YOUR LEGISLATORS WON'T PROTECT YOU.[101]

Across the top of a vacant factory closer to downtown is another message: DESTROY WHAT DESTROYS YOU—a Detroit adaptation of Langston Hughes's famed description of capitalism: "dog eat dog."[102]

Even in the West Side's semi-populated neighborhoods like the Garretts', charred houses with twisted metal roofs are remnants of recent "devil's nights" when residents torched hundreds of vacant homes. In April 2012, Detroit Mayor Dave Bing admitted that the city didn't have the money to combat arson in vacant properties and proposed letting the houses burn as long as the wind was right. The firefighter's union subsequently sued the city for negligence due to budget cuts and firehouse closures. The police officer's association has issued a warning that the department could not adequately protect the city's citizens under the strapped conditions. So many bus lines have been cut that there is always a constant stream of people walking on the sidewalk along major thoroughfares. The average high school classroom size is sixty students.[103]

"Detroit puts a human face on what is an abstract matter of property rights," said Steve Babson, a professor at Wayne State College in Michigan. "It's highly ironic when people talk about the sanctity of contracts when our understanding of contracts is so greatly flawed. This is holding sacrosanct the bank contract over all others. It's a question of whose contracts do we value?" he said.

These systemic effects of foreclosure complicate the issue of mortgage contracts. Yes, the individual houses functioned as collateral for the loans, but the survival of the neighborhoods and local city governments did not. Detroit is far from the only place on the verge of bankruptcy as a result of widespread foreclosure. Stockton, California; Central Falls, Rhode Island; and San Bernardino, California, have already declared bankruptcy under the financial weight of massive foreclosures. In San Bernandino, the local government has toyed with the idea of using eminent domain to seize mortgages in an effort to curb the never-ending downward spiral.

"It's the same pattern everywhere," said housing lawyer Jerry Goldberg. "It's just more extreme here."

Perhaps the question, then, is not whether the banks had the right to assert their individual contracts through mortgage loan repossessions, but whether they had the right to break the broader social contract through physical evictions, which cause the majority of the governmental costs and systemic issues. Housing activists and senators alike have argued for the "right to rent," which would allow families who have defaulted on their mortgages to stay in their homes and pay monthly rent. Others argue for a greater nullification of the mortgage contracts entirely, pointing to the precedent of canceling property contracts in the name of the public welfare. In the 1930s, as the Great Depression set in, twenty-seven states enacted foreclosure moratoriums, breaking the mortgage contracts to forestall a national emergency. Yet in 2013, Michigan's approach to a similar emergency was to nullify the nation's democratic contract, stripping any local electoral power away from nearly half of the state's African American population.

Bertha hired a lawyer, a "sweet man," as she describes him, to try to fight the foreclosure in court. However, because the current legal process fails to account for the systemic effects of foreclosure, there were few strategies he could bring to her defense. Bank of New York Mellon repossessed the house, and then—in the absence of buyers at the auction sale—bought it back for $12,000. That was when the lawyer told Bertha that she had to understand the reality of the situation: She'd lost her home.

At that time, a lot of people were telling Bertha the same thing. But she'd started to see the situation differently. She began thinking about a moral law, a higher law, one that surpassed lawyers and eviction notices.

"Mine was a faith-based thinking," said Bertha. "When I prayed, I could feel something turning inside me saying that I wouldn't lose this home."

Faced with this recalcitrant woman, some suggested to Michelle that her mother needed psychiatric help.

Bertha's first eviction date was November 8, 2011, only a few days after her husband returned home from another stint in the hospital. She had begun teaching him to garden as physical therapy, and she was proud that he could feel his way around their single-story house. She had continued to make a home for her husband and children, and nothing—no bank, cataracts, layoffs, or piece of paper—was going to stop her. Through negotiations with Bank of New York Mellon in October, she briefly got the company to agree to sell her the house for the $12,000, the same as the auction sale price.

But by the New Year, Bertha's troubles had only increased. In December, William went back into the hospital for brain hemorrhaging, and his brother died. She broke the news about the brother's death to William at his bedside, but she still kept the foreclosure a secret. The bank had changed its mind once again, doubling the purchasing price and then withdrawing the offer entirely. On January 26, Bertha was served with her final eviction notice, with the date set for January 30, 2012. It was less than a week away. She understood the legal reality of the situation, but she had also made up her mind.

"I can't see myself moving," she told her daughter a few nights before January 30. "How can you move a home?"

Bertha Garrett resolved to stay.

WHERE THEY GOING TO PUT ALL THESE PEOPLE?

Michael Hutchins
Chattanooga, Tennessee

At age 26, Michael Hutchins moved into his own apartment in College Hill Courts. It was on the second floor of a squat brick row house ringed by a laundry line and a cement front stoop. He had his own walk-through kitchen, a private bedroom, and a little living room in which he displayed his two most prized possessions: the framed original of his Howard High School graduation certificate and a photo of his junior-year track team. He took pride in his space, saving the leftover money from his disability checks so that he could afford to buy a small television and a couch. He mostly kept to himself and stayed inside. Hettie remembers that her son was worried that people were looking at him because he walked funny and had little control over his right arm. His speech, too, was slow, and he still often forgot specific words. For the first few years, he didn't talk to his neighbors all that often. He simply watched the people gather for afternoon football games and the annual summer barbecue on the central quad, thinking that maybe someday he'd join in.

Michael's apartment was one of 497 units, making College Hill Courts one of the largest public housing developments in the city when he first moved in 1998. It was the anchor of the Westside neighborhood, a small pocket of Chattanooga just west of downtown. As a result of urban renewal, the entire Westside is cut off from the rest of the city—and all of its jobs, stores and services—by two curved highways. In 2010, the median annual income of Westside residents was just over $9,400, and exactly 100 percent of the children were living in poverty.[104]

The history of College Hill Courts is the quintessential story of public housing in the twentieth-century United States. Built in 1941, the project traces the great failure of the for-profit housing market of the 1930s, the struggle for a new model, the rise of public housing, the disinvestment under President Nixon, and the frenzied threat of demolition since President Clinton. Yet, the history of College Hill Courts is much more than the chronicle of a public housing project. It is also a contested story about the country's changing labor force and the money and power behind the United States' addiction to mortgaged houses. Simply put, for the for-profit model to rise to such spectacular dominance by the end of the twentieth century, the public housing vision introduced early in the century had to fall. And millions of people who weren't profitable to house—people like Michael Hutchins—had to fall with it.

Before College Hill Courts was built, there were alleys to sleep in. That's how Helen Kelley, a Chattanooga resident who lived through the Great Depression, remembers it.

"Don't you know we didn't have anything like this," Kelley told the *Chattanooga Times Free Press* as she gestured at the walls of her public housing tower in south Chattanooga. "We all lived in alleys."[105]

The Great Depression created one of the worst housing crises in U.S. history. In the cities, displacement was rampant. By 1933, banks foreclosed on an average of 1,000 homes every single day. By 1934, nearly half of all urban mortgage holders had fallen behind on their payments and were at risk of eviction.[106]

In rural areas, the situation was even more dire, because foreclosure meant the loss of families' livelihoods along with their homes. Eliza Edwards, another Chattanooga resident, remembers working in the fields alongside her family members in the Depression's aftermath. She was only a child—she'd been born the year the market collapsed—but in those days, everyone in a sharecropping family worked. During the 1930s, her family's annual income was $300—about $5,000 a year in 2012 dollars.

By the early 1930s, people in both cities and rural areas had mobilized against the continued onslaught of foreclosures and evictions.

"There is an incredible history of anti-eviction organizing," said Mark Naison, a professor at Fordham University and one of the nation's leading researchers about housing organizing during the Depression.

Hundreds of thousands of farmers came together to form anti-eviction and tenants' rights groups like the Farm Holiday Association in the Midwest; the Alabama Sharecroppers Union in Louisiana, Mississippi, and Alabama; and the Southern Tenant Farmers Union, which stretched from Tennessee to Texas. The groups descended on farm auctions en masse to intimidate investors and speculators and then bet on the property with absurdly low prices—a penny! A dollar!—until the property was returned to the owner. They also banded together to do eviction defense, which, in rural areas, was simple and classically Southern.

"It was people with rifles standing there and defending the house," said Naison.

In Northern cities, eviction defense teams didn't wield guns, but they were equally effective. Primarily organized by the Communist Party, hundreds and sometimes thousands of people mobilized to stop the police from evicting families in New York City, Chicago,

Detroit, Gary, Youngstown, Toledo, and other urban centers. Masses of women filled the streets and contested homes, pouring buckets of water on the police from the rooftops. The women also beat back the police officers' horses by sticking them with long hatpins from the garment district or pouring marbles into the streets. If the police were successful in moving the family's furniture out to the curb, the crowd simply broke down the door and moved the family's belongings back inside after the police had left.

"There were times that landlords were saying, 'You can't evict anymore in the Bronx. These people control the streets,'" said Naison.

By the mid-1930s, the for-profit housing model was in crisis. New construction was at a virtual standstill. Widespread rent strikes made it impossible to turn a profit on buildings across New York City. Hundreds of World War I veterans had marched on Washington and established a tent city they called Hooverville. The encampment protests—where people lived outside the private housing market—spread across the country, entirely built, governed, and populated by the displaced. One of the largest, located in Seattle, stood for ten years, housed more than one thousand residents at its peak, and held its own elections for the community's mayor.

Elected officials finally took notice.

"Shoot the banker if he comes to your farm!" declared North Dakota Governor William Langer during his 1932 election campaign.[107] Once in office, he became one of twenty-seven governors to enact a moratorium on farm or home foreclosures during the 1930s. Governor Langer even called in the National Guard to stop sheriff sales.[108]

The crisis also initiated sweeping federal legislation, the two most comprehensive being the National Housing Act of 1934, which created the Federal Housing Administration (FHA), and the Wagner-Steagall Housing Act of 1937, which created federal subsidies for public housing.

The latter legislation was designed to "head off any great outburst of protest or revolt" by the "multitudes left unemployed, impoverished, and often homeless," writes Peter Marcuse, a professor of urban planning at Columbia University.[109]

Although public housing was a system that activists had been dreaming of for more than a decade, it wasn't politically tenable until the Great Depression. Led by women intellectuals, especially author and urban strategist Catherine Bauer, a strong housing movement emerged in the 1920s. These activists recognized that the era's deplorable slum conditions were caused not by social issues but by an underlying failure in the for-profit housing market. Many of these organizers had become disenchanted with the very premise that the market system could be expected to house the entire country—especially because the situation for the country's poor was only growing worse despite a roaring economic boom.

"Private enterprise and restrictive legislation alone have proved themselves incapable of meeting the needs of small-wage earners for adequate housing," wrote Elizabeth Hughes, director of the Bureau for Social Research for Chicago in the 1920s.[110]

The most influential work to emerge from this movement was Catherine Bauer's 1934 *Modern Housing*. The book was a study of the 4.5 million units of new housing that European governments had subsidized since the end of World War I and a clear proposal for an entirely new system of housing in the United States. Advocating for homes to be built for their use value rather than their profit margins, Bauer believed that a massive ideological shift was necessary to create a better housing model.

"The premises underlying the most successful and forward-pointing housing developments are not the premises of capitalism, of inviolate private property, of entrenched nationalism, of class distinction, of governments bent on preserving old interests rather than creating new values," she wrote.[111]

Three years after the book's publication, Bauer's ideas had permeated the highest offices in Washington. She was a lead author of the Housing Act of 1937, which mandated federal funds for public housing construction. Between 1937 and 1942, the government funded the construction of 130,000 units of affordable housing in hundreds of projects across the country.[112] In 1944, President Franklin Delano Roosevelt declared a "Second Bill of Rights" during his State of the Union Address, which re-enshrined public housing as a government priority.

"We have come to a clear realization of the fact that true individual freedom cannot exist without economic security and independence. Necessitous men are not free men," he declared.

He then listed a number of "economic truths [that] have become self-evident," including "the right of every family to a decent home."[113]

Five years later, The Housing Act of 1949, enacted under President Harry Truman, approved the funds for 810,000 new units of public housing.

In 1940, the newly formed Chattanooga Housing Authority approved the construction of its first development, College Hill Courts. Built of masonry and brick, it was constructed in the popular public housing style of the era: blocks of two-story, connected brick row houses laid out like a small, gridded town. This style would later be criticized for looking unfriendly, almost like Soviet prisons, but public housing construction had strict per-unit cost caps resulting

factory workers, many of whom lived in the projects because their wages were so low. As the industrial plants were slowly shuttered—in Chattanooga and almost every city—the government grew less and less interested in subsidizing workers' housing. In 1973, Nixon declared a moratorium on new public housing construction. That same year, Congress passed Section 8, a program to push public housing residents into the for-profit housing market by offering them housing cost vouchers. President Reagan later cut the funding for public housing by nearly 80 percent, down to $7 billion a year.[119]

Meanwhile, as the manufacturing industry declined, the practice of creating wealth by leveraging the U.S. economy rose. The mortgage industry led the charge, generating incredible amounts of money by pushing white-picket-fenced homes with 30-year price tags. The national homeownership rate jumped a full 20 percent in only four decades: from 44 percent in 1940 to 64 percent in 1980.[120] Actually, homeownership is the wrong word, because few of these families actually owned their houses outright. What was really on the rise was federally subsidized mortgage indebtedness. In 1900, about 30 percent of homes had a mortgage; by 1990s, nearly 80 percent did.[121]

Curiously, the expansion of the mortgaged housing market was not all that different from the creation of public housing earlier in the century: Both were created with vast amounts of government funding. The federal government used income tax deductions and mortgage rate subsides through Fannie Mae and Freddie Mac to promote and pay for homeownership, a practice that essentially funneled taxpayer money directly into the pockets of the mortgage industry. The amount the government spent each year on these subsidies was dizzying. In the 1980s, tax breaks for mortgage-holding families increased to an annual $50 billion even as public housing funds fell to only $7 billion. By 2012, the annual expense of this subsidy topped $100 billion. Additional federal tax breaks and financial aid to a variety of industries—including real estate, insurance, oil, and finance—further spurred the expansion of a mortgaged economy, inspiring one team of scholars to call suburbanization and the rise of homeownership "the largest welfare program in American history. . . falsely remembered as a golden age of the private market."[122]

Yet the people who stood to profit from homeownership were different from those who benefited from public housing. Homeownership subsidies overwhelmingly went to large corporations and wealthy families, and a powerful lobbying force coalesced around the expansion of the mortgaged-housing model. In contrast, public housing residents and advocates had almost no lobbying force or political clout to push the continuation of their model. With no need for factory workers, a rapidly expanding mortgage industry, and little political pressure to continue funding housing for the nation's most vulnerable, the government decided on a new course of action for public housing: run the developments into the ground, blame the residents for the failure, and then sell off the remains of the program to private industry.

By the Clinton era, the government's new approach had succeeded. Public housing was widely regarded as a failed social experiment. The divestment had physically destroyed a number of developments. At one residence, the Henry Horner Homes in Chicago, dozens of dead cats and dogs were found floating in the basement of a building.[123] But even more important, the relentless propaganda pushing the theory that public housing bred the so-called culture of poverty had fully permeated American society.

"Politically, HUD is about as popular as smallpox," a *Washington Post* article declared in 1995.[124] That same year, Congress repealed the one-to-one replacement rule, which had required that any public housing unit torn down had to be replaced. A frenzied demolition began.

There was only one problem. Inside the projects, many of the residents actually considered public housing a great success.

"I love it now," said Michael. "I really do."

As he settled into College Hill Courts over the years, Michael grew to feel comfortable and secure in his new home. His apartment was small and old, but it was well built. There had been a major renovation the year before he moved in, and his apartment had brand-new windows and doors. A few years later, the CHA also repaired the electrical wiring and plumbing. There was plenty of work to be done, but it wasn't that bad.

He joined a group of men who played dominos outside, and he began to socialize with his neighbors. The neighbors always had dogs around, and he used to save chicken bones for them.

In the afternoon, he walked across the street from College Hill Courts and volunteered at the child-care center. Michael had a way with the children; he took after his mother, who had worked in day care for years. He enjoyed being helpful, he said, and it gave him a way to give back to the community. Over the summer, he began attending the neighborhood's annual barbecue.

Michael Hutchins wasn't the only one to find College Hill Courts a supportive social environment. Close-knit communities formed there, complete with the love and rivalries of large extended families. At College Hill Courts, some older men explained that they called each other not by their first names, but by their mothers' maiden names, "in memory" of the old days when the now-deceased women lived with them in the same apartments.

Many people who reside in public housing say that these long-term support networks are the best thing about living there—and the part that the newspapers always seemed to leave out.

"When you hear public housing [in the media] you think gunshots, fires, crimes, and drugs, and murders, and killings. But they also do not tell you that the next-door neighbor is there for you. They got your back," one public housing resident in Miami explained to a team of researchers who spoke to more than seventy public housing residents in six cities. "These projects—they are considered a family. We call these projects home. That is what people really need to know."[125]

Damaris Reyes, a longtime public housing resident in New York City and the executive director of the Good Old Lower East Side, one of the nation's longest-established public housing advocacy organizations, agrees.

"I see public housing as one of the most successful New Deal and twentieth-century programs," she said. "I've always wanted to change the perception of public housing, who lives in it, and what it brings to a city."

In Chattanooga, the demolition season started with a bang. In 2002, the city tore down the Spencer J. McCallie Homes, then the city's largest public housing development. After $35 million in Hope VI grants—a federal program to turn public housing into mixed-income developments with private residences alongside public housing—McCallie reopened. Only a quarter of McCallie's former residents were allowed to return. In 2005, the city demolished the Reverend H.J. Johnson Apartments and the Maurice Poss Homes. In 2010, the Fairmount Avenue Apartments fell. The following year, the Chattanooga Housing Authority announced that Harriet Tubman, the second-largest public housing complex in the city and Michael's childhood home, would be sold. City officials wanted to tear it down, but the CHA realized it didn't even have enough funds to pay for a wrecking ball.

In other cities, the scale of the demolition was even worse. In 2000, Chicago launched a "Plan for Transformation" that destroyed 25,000 units of public housing. Atlanta made headlines by setting the goal of becoming the first city in the United States to demolish all of its large public housing complexes. Using hurricane Katrina as an excuse, New Orleans closed down almost 5,000 public housing units at a time when the city desperately needed housing. As the 2008 foreclosure and eviction crisis began, more people than ever needed the safety net of public housing. But nationally, the demolition of the projects only accelerated.

The government's solution to the demolition of public housing, the Section 8 voucher program passed under President Nixon, embodies the contradictions and failures of privatizing the government's responsibilities. It costs the government more to give a person a Section 8 voucher than to maintain a public housing unit.[126] Public housing advocates widely consider the program to be a handout for private landlords. But the biggest issue is that the vouchers create massive instability for many former public housing residents—including people right in Michael's neighborhood.

Marline Greene, a mother of three, is considered one of Chattanooga's lucky low-income residents, because after her eviction from public housing she received Section 8. The vouchers expire after a short period of time, so Greene scrambled to find a landlord willing to accept the subsidy. She found one, but the banks foreclosed on her landlord, so she and her family had to move out or be evicted by force. She found another apartment and quickly moved in. Within months, the house had neither heat nor electricity. Pieces of plaster fell from the ceiling. Rats scurried in the corners and the walls. The police later said the house should have been condemned.

But Greene knew it was too risky to move; landlords are not required to take Section 8 vouchers, so demand is fierce for the few houses that do. So Marline Greene simply tried to make the apartment livable. She slipped cardboard underneath the rug to try to level the sagging floor. The entire family slept in the kitchen with extra blankets and kerosene lamps to stay warm. Less than a year after moving in, the landlord informed her that the house was in foreclosure; she'd have to move again. The next day, Greene woke up, took her three children to the bus stop, stuffed her kids' clothes into bags, packed their birth certificates, her food stamp card, and other important papers into a briefcase, and left.

"You're trying to act like everything is all right when you're carrying around all your clothes," Greene recalls, forcing a laugh. That night, she and her youngest son slept on the floor of a shelter. Her older two sons moved in with their father. The family stayed separated for months while Greene searched, without success, for another landlord willing to accept her voucher. Her two older sons missed their mother and wanted to live with her, but Greene had nowhere to take them.

She remembered one afternoon when her sons called from school to ask if the family could spend just that one night together. Greene was forced to say no: She had no bus fare to use to go pick them up and no idea where she herself would sleep that evening.

"My whole life is like Russian roulette," Greene reflected.

The city's housing advocates and other public housing residents say that Greene's experience is common for those on Section 8.

"This is often what you see with below-market-rate slum landlords," said Ladonna Guffey, a case manager at one of the largest shelters in Chattanooga. Her clients are nearly always pushed into below-market-rate apartments, because the Section 8 credits are far less than the price of an apartment at fair market value—a reality that turns the federal government into one of slumlords' largest customers. Another Chattanooga public housing resident named Joe Clark compares Section 8 to "giving a person food stamps without a grocery store," because the city has so few affordable rental apartments.[127]

Chattanooga government officials are also well aware of the lack of affordable apartments in the city and the problems this scarcity causes.

"You can't find rent here in Chattanooga that you can afford with a minimum-wage job," said Richard Beeland, the press secretary for the mayor's office. "The math just doesn't add up. You have to have three jobs at minimum wage to afford housing. That's a problem."

The demolition of public housing has only exacerbated the crisis, he explained.

"We don't have as many public housing complexes to move people too, and . . . there are only so many landlords who will accept housing choice vouchers. So what do you do? Where do you go? That's a good question."

When asked if he is worried, he said, "We are, and every other city in America is too. We know there are people who won't have a place to live. So what do we do if we don't have adequate housing for everyone? Because we don't. It's not just us; it's everyone. It's a common problem."

As of 2013, Chattanooga had 1,500 people on the closed waiting list for public housing, 5,000 on the closed waiting list for Section 8, no year-round overnight city shelters, and more people than ever sleeping by the railroad tracks. The cost of renting was rising faster than in any city in the country outside New York City and San Francisco, making the for-profit market ever more inaccessible.[128] The Chattanooga Housing Authority was so vastly underfunded that its executive director, Betsy McCright, described her job as "triage."

In December 2011, a handful of Westside residents received a letter from Mayor Littlefield's office inviting them to a presentation and discussion regarding the future of College Hill Courts. Like the majority of the project's actual residents, Michael Hutchins wasn't invited. But he would soon hear the meeting's outcome: The city was proposing to close down College Hill Courts, evict the residents, and hand the property over to an Atlanta-based developer called Purpose Built, which specialized in privatizing public housing. Some of the residents would be allowed to return; the majority would get Section 8. As the rumors swirled, Michael and his neighbors wanted to know one thing: If the Courts closed, where were all these people going to go?

Many believe that answering that question is not the government's responsibility. But if the state legalizes, subsidizes, and glorifies one economic model that even government officials admit will never and could never lead to adequate housing for everyone, then whose responsibility is it?

EVERYTHING WAS EVERYWHERE

Martha Biggs and Jajuanna Walker
Chicago, Illinois

The shelter staff woke everyone up at 6:00 a.m.—sharp. There were no exceptions, even for Martha, who was working the night shift at her security job until 4:00 a.m. By 6:00, she was up and struggling to get her kids to school on two hours of sleep. And then there were the bugs—big fat insects the size of cockroaches. She'd lived in roach-infested apartments before, of course, so she began to scrub the floors with bleach and Pine-Sol like her mother had taught her, until she learned that heavy cleaning wasn't allowed in the shelter either. If the Pine-Sol didn't stop, the staff warned, Martha was out. Other residents of the city's shelter system had complained about the frequent thefts; one woman said that her most prized possession—her only photo of her deceased mother—had been lifted because it was in a gold frame.

The biggest problem for Martha was not the rules or the bugs or the thefts. It was the atmosphere. A spirited optimist underneath her street-tough exterior, Martha thought the shelter reeked of despondency and resignation. These were the last people she wanted her children around. She tried to feed her kids in their room to keep them out of the depressing cafeteria, but the staff accused her of starving them. She couldn't be a good mother here, she decided.

"A shelter is no place for kids," said Martha. "It's like jail."

Martha and her kids moved again.

Martha was her daughter Jajuanna's hero—and the only person Jajuanna knew she could count on.

"Me and my momma always stuck together," said Jajuanna. "She said no matter what, she would take care of me and get us what we need. She's never put anything above us."

Martha kept that promise, but it wasn't easy. She was constantly on the move: scouting out vacant apartments in Cabrini, searching for whatever two-bedrooms she might be able to afford, trying to convince family members to let her and her kids stay. She often worked, even though it was difficult to hold down jobs as a single mother with young children. She cleaned rooms in a pay-by-the-hour hotel where people came to turn tricks or cut cocaine. She ran maintenance for an office rental space. She served pizza at Sbarro. She watched the security cameras in the Water Tower. ("I was a snitch" is how she described it.) Throughout, her pay was never more than $12 an hour—and sometimes much less.

Martha had always dreamed of having a son. After leaving the shelter, she gave birth to another daughter, Justice, and then a baby boy named Davion. He had milky-white skin as an infant, but soon grew into a dark, handsome child who loved to be hugged.

The family bounced from house to house.

"We slept at auntie's house, at another auntie's house, at uncle's house, at our other uncle's house," remembers Jimmya. "We were moving so much, and I just wanted it to stop, but it didn't stop at all."

At one uncle's house, they all shared one room, and everyone slept in the same bed—except Jajuanna, who sometimes slipped down to the floor at night because she hated being squished. Another aunt had a front room with a pullout mattress for Jajuanna; at a third relative's, their cousin would crawl into bed with her mother, Martha's sister, so the family could have its own room. Sometimes there was no extra room, so Martha and her children all slept on the living room floor. There were some places Martha refused to bring her children. Other places were safe, such as Uncle Darrell's house, but they had to be careful to get there early enough, because he padlocked the door at night.

"When I got out of school, I always had to call my momma because I didn't know where she was at and where I had to go," said Jajuanna. "I just did what she told me to. But when she didn't answer the phone, then I didn't know where to go."

Sometimes Martha was forced to split the children up. Sometimes Jimmya and Justice went to their grandma's house; othertimes the kids could stay with their dads for a while. Wherever they went, the children had to listen to the adults complain and insult Martha. She should come pick up her kids, they said.

These words hurt Jimmya's feelings. She wanted to scream, "What do you think, that I can't understand the words coming out of your mouth?"—but she stayed silent.

Martha heard the complaints too, but there was nothing she could do. She had nowhere to take them. She herself was living in the back of her minivan. The relatives called and called, but Martha just lay down across the backseat and listened to the phone ring.

Homelessness in the United States looks like a lot of things. The most common—and narrow—perception of homelessness is of people who have been forced by circumstances to literally live outside, people like Dorothy and Rob, who constructed a small barricade out of blankets, shopping carts, cardboard, and plastic bags under the I-94 overpass in downtown Chicago. They've been living there "a minute"—they said—which in this case means about three years. Dorothy was barefoot. Rob carried one of the yellow WE FIX HOUSES signs that have cropped up like weeds since the foreclosure crisis. On the back he scribbled, MAN IN NEED.

A few underpasses away, a shirtless man wearing army fatigues paced back and forth, clutching a metal baseball bat in his left hand. He was angry and his eyes were wild. He didn't need nobody's help, he said. He was a veteran—he'd *served*. He'd been down here for a while. He is perhaps the quintessential stereotype of a person without an address: single man, veteran, slightly unhinged, possibly a substance user and threatening. If you only count people who are sleeping on the streets, in cars or in shelters, there are approximately 640,000 people in the United States each night without a home.[129]

This narrow definition of homelessness, however, obscures the vast number of people like Martha and her children who are forced into shifting and unstable living situations out of economic necessity. Moreover, this restricted focus often makes homelessness appear to be a social issue, one that is caused more by individual problems like mental disorders or substance abuse than by systemic issues like economic inequality or the for-profit housing model.

As Loyola University professor Talmadge Wright explains in his book *Out of Place*, categorizing people who have nowhere to live as a class that is altogether separate from those who are low-income "moved the political agenda away from issues of poverty, redevelopment, displacement, land use policies, job loss *and other structural features of capital* to those agendas generated by perceivable behavioral differences within a destitute population and the problems associated with creating better service networks" (emphasis mine).[130]

In other words, this narrow perception of homelessness makes it easy to pretend that it is these people—rather than the economic system—that are fucked up.

The Biggs family never looked "homeless," not under the narrow definition anyway. Jimmya and Justice with the stick-skinny legs of growing girls, baby Davion who always wanted to be picked up, and Jajuanna who looks so much like her mother that people addressed them as sisters on the street—they always looked clean and well fed. But before they were even teenagers, the kids had lived in so many places, they couldn't even keep track.

If you count families like the Biggses, people who are doubled up with relatives and shifting from house to house because they can't afford a place to live, there are nearly seven million people in the United States without homes.[131] Martha Biggs's best friend, Trisha James, was also living in this type of situation: a small, in-foreclosure house almost entirely devoid of furniture and without indoor plumbing. On any given night, around ten adults stayed there, along with a rotating cast of their children. The last place James had lived consistently, about a year earlier, was an apartment funded by a city program. Her building was in foreclosure, although neither she nor anyone at the assistance program knew about the pending eviction until the sheriff came to remove James and her kids two days before Christmas. Neighborhood boys set the vacant building aflame a few weeks later—before James had even had time to come back and collect her things.

James is part of a growing phenomenon of chronic, intergenerational homelessness. She, her parents, and her children all go through life each day without stable or safe places to live. The family members struggle to provide for each other, and failure adds emotional trauma to all the other hardship.

James's mother, Helen, is sick with untreated hemorrhoids that cause daily bleeding. Her goal is simple: "I just don't want to die," she said.

Yet what she speaks about the most is the feeling of not being able to provide for her children, and then not having them provide for her. The way she described sleeping on a bench during the

Chicago winter had nothing to do with the cold or the physical danger.

"It feels like nobody loves you," she said.

If nothing changes, it is likely that Trisha James's grandchildren—Helen James's great-grandchildren—won't have a home either.

"There's a generational curse on a person," said Maime Fenner, the director a shelter for women and children on the South Side of Chicago, speaking about young people who grow up without stable places to live. "But it can be broken. . . . Somebody got to break it."

Martha finally landed a good job at the Scott Petersen hot dog factory on the far West Side of the city. Established in 1927, Petersen is one of the few proud factories left in Chicago, although it is now owned by a Virginia-based company. Working the line, Martha earned enough to rent part of a two-family house on the West Side. Her landlord's bank would soon begin the process to repossess the building and foreclose the property, but she didn't know that yet.

One afternoon Martha's kids called her while she was at work to say that Jajuanna had run away. Martha left her shift and rushed home. She knew she would be fired, but her kids came first. Jajuanna, however hadn't *really* run away—at least, that's how she tells the story. She'd merely gotten fed up with babysitting and had left to take a walk around the block without telling anyone. She was gone from the house for less than an hour, she estimated.

Martha lost her job. Later, when the family was evicted from that house by a squad of police officers, Jajuanna thought it was her fault.

That day wasn't the first time Jajuanna felt responsible for things outside her control.

"I thought it was my fault we got put out of all those houses," she said later. "It was only me and my sisters and I was the oldest, so I thought it just had to be us getting Momma kicked out."

Jajuanna and Justice loved school because it was an escape.

"I love school more than anything," Jajuanna would say.

She and her sister both felt at home in the classroom, because they were bright and excelled in their course work. Yet the two were lucky that they were smart and outgoing, because switching schools became part of their September ritual. By the time Jajuanna reached high school, it was her fifth school. Jimmya's experience was even more hectic. By the time she'd reached sixth grade, she'd attended five different schools, including kindergarten, in only seven years.

The grades of most children suffer if they are forced to shuffle from school to school and struggle to find a quiet place to do their homework. But with their natural smarts and under their mother's obsessive watch, Jajuanna and Jimmya thrived academically.

"I just did my homework in the car. Or at the house we were staying at. Or I went to school early," Jimmya said. Jimmya's sixth-grade teachers would encourage the school to promote her directly to eighth grade. By the end of Jajuanna's ninth-grade year, she would have a 3.5 grade point average.

But no matter how much they loved school, their need for a place to live invaded everything. Even Jajuanna's middle school graduation day was almost ruined. Jajuanna was a talented singer and she loved to perform. She'd been chosen to sing a solo of "Children Hold on to Your Dreams." She was so excited; she knew she could hit all the high notes, and she was graduating with all A's and B's. But before the ceremony began, she broke down crying. Would her mom be able to come? Would she find a ride? Would something come up?

When she saw Martha in the audience, wielding a borrowed video camera and a wide smile, Jajuanna was so happy. Still, her sisters and brother weren't there. Davion was with his father, and Jimmya and Justice with their grandmother. Martha hadn't been able to get hold of them.

The performance was one of the highlights of Jajuanna's life, even though her siblings couldn't make it. She didn't blame them for their absence; she knew they were all experiencing the same thing. Justice was also aware that her transient home life made being successful at school more difficult.

"When I was homeless, it wasn't like I was dirty because my mom made sure I wasn't. But then I was going to school with everything on my mind of what happened the other night—that yesterday I got to a house, but what about today? I might have to sleep in the car today. I might get a good meal today. But will I get a meal? Will something go wrong? What will happen? How will I get home today? Will he open the door at night? . . . When I was nine, it was so hard. I asked Momma, 'Why we at uncle Dunny's house so much?' I asked, 'Why did the police take over our house?' " Martha Biggs calmed her children—and herself.

"We're going to get something better," she promised the girls.

As Martha's dreams began to look more and more like fantasies, so too did Chicago's promises for many residents on the South and West Sides. As in Detroit, the wave of foreclosures was creating deep systemic issues, and the worst was the crime. For some, it began to look as if Chicago itself was a city of dreams deferred.

"It's like Iraq out here," said a man named Jack, who was sitting on the front steps of a house in Woodlawn, a neighborhood on the South Side.

Indeed, throughout the course of the ten-year war, the number of U.S. soldiers killed in Iraq has topped the number of murders in Chicago during only the four bloodiest years of war (2004–2007).[132] During all others, the number of Chicagoans killed in the city's streets outpaced the number of U.S. soldiers killed in Iraq—an active war zone.

Woodlawn's murder rate is lower than neighborhoods like Inglewood, and the vacancy is less than in places like Roseland, which Jack called "the Wild Hundreds." Still, the neighborhood is pockmarked with vacant, burnt-out, and boarded-up buildings. On an average block there were about three vacant two- or three-story houses, and sometimes as many as six or eight—nearly a third of the street. On the homes that were occupied, many displayed a small sign tucked into the screen door: DON'T SHOOT, read the lettering superimposed on a child's face. I WANT TO GROW UP.

Most of the foreclosed houses were already stripped clean of anything that could be sold for scrap, such as a Bank of America-owned two-family house where the plumbing had been torn out of the walls and the carpet was stained with watermarks. There were no signs of the bank fulfilling its requirement to secure and maintain the house except for a sign that read: ENTRY BY UNAUTHORIZED PERSONS IS STRICTLY PROHIBITED. The basement door was unlocked and wide open.

One house had a gaping hole where the exterior wall of the third floor belonged. Arson in vacant buildings was a growing problem for the Chicago Fire Department. In 2011, two firefighters died trying to extinguish a flame at a vacant, foreclosed building that had fallen into hazardous disrepair. In other cities, bank-foreclosed properties have posed lethal hazards, particularly when looters strip gas pipes only to learn that the banks had neglected to turn off the gas. Some houses burn; others explode.

Another house had a basement filled with piles of trash, clothes, dusty Hula Hoops and empty Cobra vodka bottles. It reeked of tuna fish.

"Did you know they killed someone in that backyard just this morning?" the next-door neighbor said. His voice lacked emotion; the shooting appeared to be an unsurprising occurrence.

The housing activists in Chicago brave enough to investigate these vacant bank-owned properties tell battle stories.

"There was one [vacant] house we canvassed in Englewood, and two weeks later a 16-year-old girl got shot in the front yard," said Loren Taylor, who works with Occupy Homes Chicago.

Thomas Turner, director of a new nonprofit, Help House Chicago's Homeless, remembers seeing the inside of one PNC-owned house.

"There were feces in the basement, urine, rolled up carpet," he began. "It was abandoned for six years, so squatters and strippers had punched holes in the walls. There was no toilet, no tub, all the kitchen cabinets were torn out. The bedroom looked like someone had taken a sledgehammer and just started swinging. . . . I still see gang members on the front porch or rolling up real slow in the car." According to his conversations with the neighbors, the former owner of the house had been an elderly man—eighty or ninety years old.

Another Chicago resident, Erica Johnson, provides a similar description of a vacant home: "There were clothes, books, broken dressers, little white drug bags, used condoms. . . . It was a little drug house, and they were probably bringing their girls up in here," she said.

The banks are required to maintain and market their foreclosed properties, but they often shirk their responsibility, especially in minority neighborhoods like those in the South Side of Chicago. In April 2012, the National Fair Housing Alliance filed a complaint with the U.S. Department of Housing and Urban Development and another against Wells Fargo after a two-year investigation in ten cities revealed that bank-owned houses in communities of color were far less likely to have proper for-sale signs, cut grass, trash-free lawns, and up-to-code renovations. Homes in neighborhoods of color were, for example, 82 percent more likely to have broken or boarded-up windows. Cities have increased fines levied against banks that don't maintain upkeep on their houses, but not a single bank has been held accountable for the murders and rapes that occur on their properties.

The problem extends far beyond Chicago. In Los Angeles, at least one home owned by Deutsche Bank became a brothel. The walls upstairs advertised the girls, whose names and prices had been scrawled in blue marker. Neighbors told a reporter that during the day, the girls brought in and out of the unsecured house looked like twelve- to sixteen-year-old children.[133] In the suburbs, sophisticated indoor marijuana farms and organized crime syndicates are increasingly operating out of former million-dollar homes, according to the Drug Enforcement Administration.[134]

On a tour of the crack houses in Minneapolis, certified building inspector Dorian Morris explained how a family's home turns into a drug den. First, the bank forecloses on a home and the sheriff evicts the family if the residents haven't already left. (In other states, the eviction is carried out by a bailiff, a constable or the police department, depending on local laws.) Once it is empty, the bank sends a contractor to seal up and winterize the house. Next, the strippers come in, sometimes gaining access by kicking in the small windows in the stonewall foundations of older homes, other times breaking the locks. They rarely rip the boards off the windows; those are secured by hex-screws, which require a special type of wrench to loosen. Inside, they strip the house of the copper wiring, the plumbing and sometimes even the furnace. The copper alone can bring looters anywhere from 50 cents to a dollar per pound. Outside, they tear the aluminum siding right off the house if they're desperate. Finally, people dealing drugs—in Minneapolis, that means mostly crack—begin to use the house at night as a distribution center, since it's already open. In places like Ohio, foreclosed homes more often become meth labs; in the suburbs of California, they are used mostly for growing marijuana.

Back in Chicago, the crime fostered by these vacant, foreclosed properties has grown so pervasive that, just after the city's murder rate caused a scandal during the summer of 2012, Mayor Rahm Emanuel announced that the city would spend $4 million tearing down two hundred of the worst properties. To Martha, the announcement sounded like a cruel joke: pouring millions into tearing down buildings when thousands of the city's residents didn't have a place to live.[135] After the Biggses' eviction from the foreclosed West Side apartment, Martha promised her children that things would get better, but they just got worse. The family moved into another foreclosed building, and then, finally, into their old white minivan. Jajuanna was in sixth grade at the time. She remembers how everyone slept: "My mom and I got the front seats, so we'd let the seats down all the way back. But my legs would hurt in the front so sometimes I'd lie down all the way in the back seat and Jimmya would switch with me in the front. Davion and Justice would take the seats right behind the driver."

Jajuanna hated that she couldn't stretch out her legs, but everyone adapted as best they could. They learned that they had to stop giving Davion water after 7:00 p.m.; otherwise, he'd pee all over himself and the car at night. Martha stored golf clubs and baseball bats in the car, just in case. The rest of the family's larger belongings she stored with friends or family members, who sometimes kept the possessions they liked best, such as Jajuanna's and Jimmya's bikes.

At night, Jajuanna watched her mother cry.

"She tried to hide it, and I acted like I didn't see anything. If I was laying down in the car and I saw her in the mirror, I'd just act like I was asleep. She always put her hands on her face," she said.

As the oldest, Jajuanna felt increasing pressure and responsibility for her family's situation. Her younger siblings were too little to understand. They'd often cry to their mother that they wanted to go home, pleas that Martha didn't know how to answer.

"I saw my momma struggle more than anyone," said Jajuanna. "And making it worse was that she had all of us, and that she couldn't go anywhere because she didn't trust people around us. Mom just kept moving. We just kept moving."

Finally, one night when Jajuanna was in seventh grade, she cracked. She took box cutters to her hands and wrists, making shallow slices in her skin. She'd heard about cutting from other girls at school, but she didn't really know how it worked. She was aiming for a vein, she said later, but she missed. The next day, in the bathroom at school, she tried again.

"It was because of all the things we were going through. I just didn't want to do it anymore. I thought it would be better if I were gone," Jajuanna remembers.

Martha understood what had happened—and why.

"My daughter Jajuanna damn near tried to kill herself," she said years later. "She's got welts on her forearm because she thought it was her fault."

Jajuanna began getting counseling at school. She also began to write, filling notebooks upon notebooks with poetry, song lyrics, and journal entries, which she shared with her teachers and principal, who wrote notes back to her. But the emotional support didn't change the daily reality.

A year passed with little change. The Biggses continued sleeping in the car until someone called Department of Child and Family Services to report seeing children sleeping in a white minivan. Martha knew the kids had to be split up again. They went to live with their fathers or grandparents.

One afternoon, Martha confided in her friend Patricia Hill, a retired police officer who worked with the Chicago Anti-Eviction Campaign. Martha knew all about the Campaign; she'd grown up with the group's founder, J.R. Fleming, in Cabrini. She'd heard that the group had saved Hill's house from foreclosure, so Martha told Hill about the car, about DCFS, told her she needed to do something. Anything.

"How much do you want to do something?" the woman asked her friend. The Chicago Anti-Eviction Campaign had been talking about a strategy to deal with all these families without homes and all these empty houses, a way to solve two problems at the same time—and take back some control of the neighborhood.

"Enough to not be sleeping in my car," Martha replied.

Hill stared at Martha hard for a moment and handed her a set of keys.

THE FIGHT

They have taken our houses through an illegal foreclosure process, despite not having the original mortgages.

—*The Declaration of the Occupation of New York City, accepted by the NYC General Assembly September 29, 2011*

Detroit Wins
When We Win
And Fucking Live
Here

—*Poem scrawled on a bathroom stall at bar in Detroit*

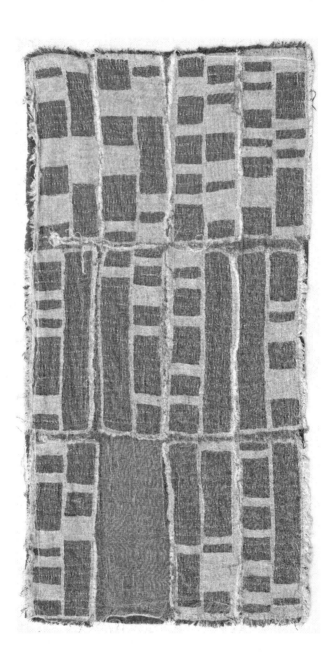

Foreclosure Quilt representing Detroit, Michigan, by Kathryn Clark. Made from cheesecloth, linen, cotton and quilting thread; 22" x 44".

WE ARE THE . . .

Griggs Wimbley
Sanford, North Carolina

Griggs filled an entire box of the mail-certified letters that he'd sent to senators, the governor, the FBI and even President Obama. All of his correspondence contained warnings about fraud and pleas for help. No one wrote back. He was tired of feeling alone and ignored, and he was bursting with information and knowledge about the illicit secrets of the foreclosure crisis. He began talking to others in the area, offering to review their paperwork to see if their foreclosures looked suspicious. He wasn't surprised to find that the majority did. And it wasn't until much later that he realized how powerful—and dangerous—the information he held actually was.

One woman he met was named Marcella Robinson. In her mid-thirties, Robinson had a striking presence. She was quite tall, with an angular face and a forceful voice. She was new to North Carolina, and she still had more of the Washington, D.C., edge than the easygoing cadence of the suburban almost-South. Robinson had left her corporate job and moved from the urban capital to a neighborhood outside of Raleigh in 2008 so her three kids could grow up in the picket-fence lifestyle. Her subdivision was perfect, filled with gently curving streets with names like Smooth Stone Trail and Dove Tree Lane and lined by stately homes with pitched roofs and brick facades and Cape Cod-style clapboard shutters. From the outside, her neighborhood looked like exactly the type of subdivision that Griggs would have liked to build, before he got ensnared in his own foreclosure.

But there was a catch: The building company that created the community had an agreement with Countrywide, the nation's largest pusher of mortgages. Robinson bought one of the company's last predatory loans before Countrywide fell apart under the weight of its toxic assets and was subsumed into Bank of America. Less than two years after moving to the suburbs, Robinson was in foreclosure.

When Griggs reviewed Robinson's paperwork he found evidence of robo-signing and other types of fraud. Robinson wasn't surprised. She'd been feeling cheated since the foreclosure process began. But she was new to the neighborhood and hesitant to say anything. Besides, the suburbs of North Carolina are not places where people talk openly about foreclosure. But one day, Robinson let it slip. It was the fall of 2010, and she was pregnant and gardening in her front yard. One of her neighbors' sons stopped to exclaim that he was surprised to see a late-term pregnant woman bent over and her hands in the dirt. Robinson told him that gardening was soothing, and that she was under a lot of stress because of problems with the bank. She was having trouble sleeping, and she'd started to feel uncomfortable in her own home. (Later, the fear would become so debilitating that she slept with a baseball bat under her bed just for the sense of security.)

The boy replied that his mother, Nicole Shelton, was stressed about the exact same thing. Robinson reached out, and Shelton explained that she'd missed a payment two years earlier after her husband had been in a car crash. She was scared; she ran a day-care business out of her house, and she had three children and an injured husband. An eviction would destroy everything. Griggs found evidence of fraud in Shelton's paperwork, too.

Robinson and Shelton began knocking on doors in their subdivision and hosting foreclosure support meetings throughout the spring and summer of 2011, which Griggs attended. They held the first meeting in the backyard of Shelton's house, gathering outside because Shelton and her family had already been evicted from their home. At the time of the first meetings, Shelton, her husband, and her three children were bouncing between a shelter, cheap hotels, and relatives' houses. Shelton was in the midst of what she later called a "catatonic" breakdown.

The meetings made a big impression on Griggs. Up to fifty people from the community attended, and Griggs felt he had a responsibility to help however he could.

"I just felt that I could feel their pain, and I knew they felt helpless," he said.

He often offered to review other families' paperwork. The community members soon coalesced into a group called Mortgage Fraud NC, and at meetings they began to discuss what they could do about this onslaught of foreclosures and Nicole's repossessed home.

Meanwhile, all across the country similar groups of people began meeting throughout that spring and summer of 2011. Griggs didn't know about these meetings; he was undergoing double knee surgery and preoccupied by the situation in North Carolina. But as he watched news coverage of August's street protests in London, in which frustrated youth fought back against mass unemployment and violent policing, he suspected the outcry would soon reach the United States.

Griggs was right. Just as he and Robinson's neighbors were brainstorming ways to resist foreclosure in suburban North Carolina, groups of people who shared Griggs's deep disillusionment with the imbalance of power in the United States were planning for action. They were inspired by the rebellions sweeping across the Middle East and around the world. Students were taking over their universities in Chile. *Los indignados* ("the outraged") were

Thousands gather to liberate a vacant, foreclosed home in East New York, Brooklyn, on December 6, 2011. Photo by Michael Gould-Wartofsky

gathering in Madrid. Mass protests were mobilizing in Greece. Youth were rebelling on the streets of London. Even in Madison, Wisconsin, teachers had organized and taken over the state capitol for weeks. It seemed as if in all corners of the earth millions of people were gathering, speaking out, and rising up to challenge those in power. The whole world seemed to be edging closer to the revolutionary possibilities of real democracy.

On September 17, more than one thousand people converged on the financial district in downtown Manhattan. Some came to participate in a single event: the U.S. Day of Rage, a protest against corporate money in politics. Others came to launch an indefinite occupation of the financial district. As the people marched, they were pushed by the police off Wall Street and ended up congregating in nearby Zuccotti Park. That night, they held an arduous general assembly in which everything was decided by open discussion and debate. A consensus was reached to spend the night in the park.

Within weeks, protests or encampments exploded in all corners of the country and world: in Oakland, Little Rock, Winnipeg, Auckland, Oslo, Seoul—even in the streets of Ulaanbaatar, Mongolia. Protesters camped out in igloos in Anchorage, Alaska. By the end of October, one reporter estimated that there were more than two thousand occupied zones worldwide.[136]

Griggs watched the protests from afar in awe. He ached to fly to New York to join in. But his surgery had left him unable to march, and he knew that there was work to be done not just on Wall Street but also along the winding roads closer to home. Others realized that too, and Occupy meetings soon sprang up in the nearby cities of Raleigh, Durham, Greensboro, and Winston-Salem.

From the outset, the housing crisis was one of the main grievances of the Occupy movement, and the reclamation of land was a core strategy for protest. Because the banks' actions were responsible for the collapse, foreclosures were one of the best representations of the system's chronic injustice: Predatory bankers got rewarded with trillion-dollar bailouts, while their victims received eviction notices. It is no coincidence that the most recognizable symbol of the Occupy movement, a tent, is a form of shelter. Housing is the personal made political. Homes are both the symbolic and the real sites of Wall Street's injustice. On December 6, 2011, a coalition of new and preexisting housing organizations unified under the name Occupy our Homes to launch simultaneous actions in more than twenty-five cities.

Mortgage Fraud NC wasn't ready for action in December, and the group kept planning throughout the winter, even as Occupy encampments were themselves evicted by local police forces, acting under the direction from Homeland Security, in cities across the country. Finally, on April 6, 2011, Griggs Wimbley and dozens of other neighbors and community members converged on Nicole Shelton's repossessed home in the first acts of civil disobedience against foreclosure in the state since the economic collapse began. While he and others gathered in the driveway, some entered and reoccupied the home that had sat vacant, unused, and bank-owned for nearly one year—the same year in which Shelton and her family had had no place to live. Griggs watched what he'd already known become a reality: The banks didn't own these homes. That was just a lie, one rooted in hundreds, thousands of other little lies and corruptions that Griggs had carefully uncovered. The people owned these homes.

"It was just an unbelievable scene," said Griggs.

But Griggs soon learned that acting on this knowledge could be a dangerous affair. He watched as twenty police officers and an eight-person SWAT team marched down the street toward the house in two perfectly straight lines. Griggs thought they looked more like the U.S. military than part of the Raleigh police department, especially because the SWAT team members were carrying M5 submachine guns. A helicopter roared overhead.

"Do you work for Wells Fargo now?" a woman from the crowd yelled.

On the police's orders, Griggs, Robinson, and Shelton all left the driveway of her home. The police arrested seven neighbors—many of whom were active members of local Occupy movements—who refused to leave.

Griggs still believed it was a successful action, even though it didn't lead to a permanent reoccupation of Shelton's home. He and others saw the truth—even if it was temporary. Attending Mortgage Fraud NC's meetings and watching protests explode across the United States had been cathartic for Griggs. He no longer felt lost or alone. He'd begun to feel like what he'd learned in the last ten years of his life was no longer a curse but a gift: a devastating story that he could share with others so that hopefully, maybe, things would change.

"I'm just so blessed and fortunate that I learned all this," he said. "I can see something really beautiful come from the things I've gone through. I'm really at peace now."

Griggs still doesn't have any faith in the American system. He foresees more devastation and collapse in store for the United States economy, since he knows that power and wealth are even more concentrated than before the collapse. Nevertheless, he remains committed to doing everything he can to stop it.

"I'm going to have a new beginning, and I'm looking forward to it. I'm going to help a lot of people," he said.

He now dreams of starting his own bank centered on low interest rates and honest practices. It would take more money that he's got—far more money—and he knows that.

Still, it feels good to start dreaming again.

CALL OFF THE DOGS

Bertha Garrett
Detroit, Michigan

The day of the Garretts' eviction began as an unforgiving Michigan morning. It was bitterly cold, about 25 degrees Fahrenheit. The roads were so slick that a driver on the East Side had already crashed into a utility pole and died before most of the city even woke.[137] On Bertha and William's street, an inch of packed snow blanketed the front yards and roofs of the neighborhood, and ice tinged the branches of the leafless trees. The whole world looked grey and bleak, except for Bertha and William's front lawn. It was buzzing with energy.

A small crowd had amassed, the freezing people stamping their feet and hunching over small cups of steaming coffee that were delivered by Bertha's neighbors. Willie and Tommy McDade from up the street were there, Willie wrapped in a purple-and-yellow-checkered scarf. A.J. Freer, the vice president of the United Auto Workers Local 600, mingled with a handful of workers from his union. A younger crowd, some sporting Occupy Detroit patches, clustered together, talking about the plans. One driver with the Teamsters Union had arrived at 4:30 a.m. just in case things got started early.

The action had been thrown together at nearly the last moment, and no one knew how it would play out. The previous Friday—only three days earlier—Michelle had called Eric Campbell, a reporter at the *Michigan Citizen*, to explain the impending eviction. Campbell started making calls. Bertha, meanwhile, finally told her husband, William, about the eviction and her and Michelle's plan to fight it. He agreed.

"Just telling me I got to up and leave . . . I just can't see it," he said. "I can't understand it. We got a lot of love in this house. We watch out for each other. I can walk the street over here, being a blind man, and I feel pretty secure," he paused as his voice caught in his throat. "I get a little emotional, because everybody watches out for me ... I just can't see walking away from what I've worked for for years. I just can't do it. I'm tired of seeing the bank and the mortgage companies distress this Detroit. I'm not going to walk away from this. I'm going to fight for it. I'm going to fight till my last breath."[138]

By Saturday night, all the local activist and community groups were gathered together in Bertha's home: Moratorium Now!, People Before Banks, Occupy Detroit, Jobs for Justice, and the United Auto Workers Union Local 600. Because the crisis hit Detroit earlier and harder than other places, the city has a vast network of housing groups, some of which have been at the forefront of the growing national movement since well before Occupy began. Detroit's local union branches, too, are some of the most radical of any in the country, and the UAW Local 600 had a long history of political and social activism.

"Unions used to be groups that championed social issues, not just groups that negotiated really good contracts," said A.J. Freer, the second vice president of the Local 600. He considered the effort to reestablish unions as the guardians of society to be just as important to his job as representing his own workers—both for the good of his city and for the future of unions themselves.

Still, two days didn't give the group much time to work with. Reverend Charles Williams, a prominent local pastor at King Solomon Missionary Baptist Church, organized a prayer circle for Sunday night to give Bertha courage. Others were more straightforward.

"Occupy Detroit was honest with me," said Bertha. "There was no false hope. It was last-minute, they said, but they'd try."

A truck pulling an enormous construction dumpster came rumbling down Pierson Street around mid-morning on Monday. That was the moment everyone was waiting for. In Detroit, a city ordinance states that a dumpster must be placed in front of the foreclosed house in order to proceed with the eviction, meaning that if the dumpster is blocked, so too is the process of evicting people from their homes. As the truck approached, one car, and then a second, screeched to a stop in the middle of the street, parking laterally to prevent the dumpster from reaching the house. A young man ran down the road and jumped onto the driver's side of the truck, shouting for him to turn around. The crowd of people rushed into the street. An older man with Parkinson's disease planted himself in front of the truck's bumper and shook his fist.

"It was crazy," remembers Joe McGuire, a law student who worked with Occupy Detroit. "It's one thing to know academically [what a blockade is], but to see it is another thing."

The driver circled the block, trying to park the dumpster nearby. But Bertha's neighbors were prepared. One man told the driver that he couldn't park that shit in front of his house. Others agreed. Blocked and confused, the driver finally left.

Michael Shane, one of Bertha's neighbors and an organizer with Moratorium Now!, called Bertha to tell her that the dumpster had left—for now.

As neighbors and supporters blocked the dumpster from reaching her house, Bertha stood in a hallway inside the imposing Dime Building in Detroit's downtown financial district. Completed in 1912, the building is a twenty-three-story steel-frame skyscraper initially named after its first primary tenant, the Dime Savings Bank. In 2009, it was renamed the Chrysler Building when executives at the auto manufacturer moved into the top two floors, but the new name didn't change the building's symbolism as Wall Street's outpost in Detroit. And in a small office on the ninth floor was Bank of New York Mellon's local headquarters.

The Bank of New York Mellon is despised in Detroit for gambling away $1 billion worth of the city's pension funds in the years leading up to the financial meltdown.[139] The bank had come under similar fire on the East Coast, where it stole nearly $2 billion from New Yorkers' pension funds, including the retirement funds of firefighters, teachers, and police, by lying to its clients about the foreign exchange rates on trades.[140] But in Detroit, the gambling loss contributed to such a budget shortfall that the local government was nearly taken over by a state receiver only months after the money's disappearance was revealed. In the ensuing debate, many mistakenly blamed the union workers themselves, rather than the bank that lost their pensions, for the city's financial crisis.

Outside of the Dime Building, about two dozen people stood shivering and holding signs reading, STOP THE EVICTION OF THE GARRETT FAMILY. Inside, Bertha was camped out on the ninth floor, waiting to speak to a representative about her mortgage contract. She had leverage now; a crowd of protesters had just turned away the city's dumpster and halted the bank's intended eviction. Yet the secretary informed Bertha that she would not be allowed in. No one was available to see her today. From the hallway, the little office looked about as far away from the center of global capital as one could get, but Bertha realized that it still operated under the same rules of exclusion and faceless bureaucracy.

"I watched the men go in and out, and I just thought: Well, if I can't go in, then they can't come out," she said.

With that thought in her mind, sixty-five-year-old Bertha Garrett, decked out in her elegant winter coat and cream-colored fur hat, lay down in front of the door to the office of the Bank of New York Mellon Corporation in the Financial District of Detroit, and she refused to move.

The term "eviction blockade" is not a metaphor. As Bertha's splayed body and the dumpster-blocking crowd demonstrate, eviction blockades are physical, embodied actions designed to prevent authorities from seizing control of a family's home. Since the housing crisis began, communities in dozens of cities across the United States have orchestrated eviction blockades that are powerful, nonviolent, and utterly magical.

"My daughter called and said that the sheriff was here," remembered Patricia Hill, a retired police officer whose eviction blockade stopped the foreclosure of her century-old two-story graystone in Chicago. "So I called J.R., and before you know it, all these people are on the porch chanting, 'Fight! Fight! Fight!' and then more people are coming up on bicycles and everyone is saying, 'We are the people—*What?*' My neighbors are out on their porches and we're yelling, 'We got a story—*What?*' The construction worker down the street is coming over, and the whole porch is filled with people chanting, 'To tell the whole wide world this is the people's territory!' And the eviction blockade is out in full force."

She paused to catch her breath. At sixty-one years old, with porcelain skin and a bun of grey dreadlocks, Hill was gracefully perched on her stone front steps more than a year after the bank attempted to evict her in March 2011.

"It was a beautiful thing. I felt like I was floating outside myself, and I was just watching all these people on my front porch to defend my home," she said.

Housing activists in the United States have used the tactic of eviction blockades for nearly a century, if not longer. Inspired by Occupy's ethos of direct action and people power, eviction blockades are once again spreading across the country as a definitive tactic of the housing movement. Drawing directly on the symbols of Occupy's encampments, some eviction blockades turn into miniature tent cities on the families' front lawns. In Atlanta, Carmen Pittman turned her grandmother's foreclosed house into a neighborhood community center, complete with a half dozen tents and an outdoor kitchen. In Center Point, Alabama, Allyn Hudson of Occupy Birmingham lived in a tent on the Ward family's front lawn for fourteen weeks during the winter of 2011—2012, weathering storm systems and a tornado that passed within one hundred feet of the tent.

Each eviction blockade has its own story. In Toledo, a man sealed himself into his own home with cinder blocks and cement, forcing the police to spend days trying to get him out. In Minneapolis, one woman defiantly planted a garden in her backyard a few weeks before her scheduled eviction to demonstrate that she was not going to leave. In New York City, waves of people halted auctions of bank-foreclosed homes by singing in the courtrooms, and more than one thousand people amassed for a home liberation in East New York, Brooklyn, on December 6, 2012. Sometimes eviction blockades are not just physical actions, but also life-changing moments of bravery.

"I've been bullied all my life," said Scot Johnson, one of the residents of the Riverdale Mobile Home Trailer Park in rural Pennsylvania. A quiet, feline-looking man, Johnson had been abused as a child by his father, he confided. Later, he was pushed around by the state, which seized his family's land to build a highway. Then the abuse came from aggressive landlords. Finally, when he heard that he was to be displaced from his trailer because a water extraction company had bought the land to expand the region's fracking industry, it was the last straw.

"As you can imagine, I'm getting tired of being pushed around by corporations, schools, the government—anyone that thinks they can push us around," he said. Rather than move, he helped run a round-the-clock eviction blockade that lasted weeks. Adjacent to the highway that bordered the park, two other blockading residents, ten-year-old twins Amanda and Chevelle Eck, painted a sign that captured the spirit of not just Johnson's experience but of all eviction blockades.

The sign read: WE ARE NOT EXPENDABLE.

Some eviction blockades go beyond signs and crowds and use "hard locks"—such as chains and bicycle locks—to make it much more difficult to move the protesters' bodies. In Minneapolis, the Cruz family defended their home from eviction for months with the help of friends, neighbors and multiple hard lockdowns. In one of the many successful defense actions, eight sheriff department officers slammed a battering ram though the front door of the house at 4:00 a.m. only to find two people locked to the peak of the house's steep shingled roof and another two with their necks locked to the bars of the second-floor balcony. All four were extricated from their locks with jackhammers and electric saws, a process that provided enough time for hundreds of neighbors to amass at the home and reoccupy it through the backdoor.

Hard lockdowns are not for the faint of heart. The most popular method is to cuff a person's neck to a structure with a bicycle

U-lock, such as the two did on the railing. Police have to sever the metal, which is only inches from one's neck, with diamond saws, jackhammers, or "jaws of life"—cutters powered by piston-rod hydraulics used to rescue people from car crashes and collapsed buildings. In the 1980s, Greenpeace began using even more secure lockboxes such as "metal sleeves" to block chemical weapons shipments. To use these devices, two people each insert one arm into a hollow tube and lock their wrists to a central rod using a carabineer, a latch device used for climbing. It can take the police hours to cut through the reinforced metal, so officers will often use "pain compliance," assaulting people with pepper spray or other types of physical and psychological abuse in an attempt to coerce them to unlock themselves. Once, police even soaked Q-tips in liquid pepper spray and swabbed it directly in protesters' eyes in an attempt to force a group of women to release themselves from their lockdown.[141]

The 4:00 a.m. raid was only one of multiple eviction attempts thwarted by the hard lockdowns at the Cruz house, which made national headlines and terrified Freddie Mac, the federally owned mortgage company that was attempting to repossess the house.

"What is unusual, in fact to our experience utterly unprecedented, is the level of aggression and defiance of the law by these activists," a spokesperson for Freddie Mac told the *Star Tribune*.[142]

During these moments, blockades throw an actual wrench in the system, temporarily halting auction sales or evictions by pitting people's bodies against the mechanisms of global capital. Yet the longer-lasting power of eviction defense actions comes from the moral crisis that they create for those who witness them. Viewers are suddenly forced to see the violence that lies at the heart of society's current housing system, evils that rarely manifest themselves because the people rarely resist.

By illuminating this moral crisis for neighbors and the larger community, eviction defense efforts can force the bankers to the negotiation table, where they must confront a community's demands. In Bertha's case, the demand was for Bank of New York Mellon to sell her the house for the auction price of $12,000. But her action was also just one piece of a growing national campaign with much bigger demands: state moratoriums on foreclosures, followed by widespread principal reduction for all home mortgage-holders.

Actions linked to these demands are gaining momentum across the country as people realize the full social and economic impacts of continued foreclosures and evictions, not just on families but

Neighbors and friends link arms around the Cruz family home in South Minneapolis during an eviction blockade in May 2012. Photo by Peter Leeman.

also on the broader society. Even the U.S. Treasury Department has come out in support of widespread principal reductions, arguing that reducing the mortgages will be less costly for the government than continuing the foreclosure process.[143]

Some housing activists fear that even such a principal-reduction plan won't fully confront the injustices of the for-profit housing system. It would act as a reset button for current mortgage-holding families, they argue, but fail to force future changes in the system. Even worse, they say that it fully ignores those in the lower third of the U.S. economy, people like Martha Biggs and Michael Hutchins, who don't have the luxury of challenging their home's foreclosure to begin with.

The theoretical power of principal reduction, however, is in demonstrating that economic contracts are not immutable, that with enough outcry and organizing, any economic reality can be renegotiated for the public good. In this sense, principal reduction would affect everyone in society, because Americans are growing increasingly indebted, not only with mortgages but also with consumer, student, and medical debt. Winning widespread principal reduction would demonstrate that enough defaults (whether intentional or by necessity), coupled with community defense teams, can force the dissolution of any type of debt. In the wake of the economic crisis, citizens of other countries have already won these types of victories. Iceland, for example, structurally reduced the mortgage debts of more than one-quarter of the country's mortgage-holding families, a reduction in loans totaling 13 percent of the country's gross domestic product.[144] Spain enacted a two-year moratorium on evictions for any family in circumstances of "extreme necessity" after a spate of suicides in 2012 that was not unlike the wave of foreclosure-related suicides that swept the country in 2011 and 2012.[145]

Many people in the United States worry that dissolving debt would cause the banks to lose confidence in borrowers, leading to sharp increases in interest rates and stringent rules for lending, which would actually make homeownership a more difficult goal to achieve. But these concerns miss the broad analysis—and are almost laughable to people like Gerardo Cajamarca, who has lost all confidence in the mortgage industry.

"Credit—they're always threatening your credit," the Minneapolis resident said in Spanish. "So I told them, 'If you don't trust me, okay. That's fine. Because I already don't trust you.'"

The real problem, Cajamarca and others argue, is the underlying system of debt-financed capitalism that portrays itself to be about freedom and ownership but is really focused on producing as much profit as possible, as fast as possible, from interest and fees generated by mass debt and related financial "products." Achieving principal reduction would be the first step toward the ultimate goal of overhauling this economic model in favor of one that does not force the majority of the population into lifelong debt. It's a lofty and seemingly impossible goal—except for those who make it happen in their own lives.

"They want you to call off the dogs," Bertha's lawyer told her over the phone the morning after the eviction blockade. It was around 9:30 a.m. on Tuesday, and Bertha was sitting at the city council building waiting to speak out against her eviction. In her front yard, an even larger crowd had amassed than the one present the day before, just in case the city tried to deliver the dumpster. But the precaution was unnecessary. Bank of New York Mellon's lawyers had called. They were tired of the articles and the phone calls; they didn't need any more bad press. If Bertha wanted the house for $12,000, she could have it.

"I'm trying to laugh, but I'm hyperventilating," Bertha remembers. For the days that followed, she could barely contain her emotions.

At a celebration in front of the house the following day, Bertha explained how she felt when she first heard that the bank's lawyers had capitulated.

"I felt like shouting. I felt like running down this street. . . . Your presence gave me strength to fight. And my daughter and my neighbors, they gave me strength to fight. And the prayers of everyone that prayed for me. So how do I feel? I feel like dancing! I feel like shouting! I feel like worshiping God, that's how I feel! I feel good! I feel like that house has been lifted off my shoulders. I feel like I can help my husband now without every day wondering: Do I tell him that he has to move? *How* do I tell him without him falling down and having a stroke? That's what I feel like."[146]

A few weeks later, Bertha signed the paperwork to buy her home back from Bank of New York Mellon for $12,000. Her whole sixty-five-year-old body felt numb as she scrawled her signature in order to finally be safe in the place that was already her home.

I WILL NOT GO BACK

Michael Hutchins
Chattanooga, Tennessee

Michael was nervous about the future of College Hill Courts.
In the winter of 2011, he often visited his mother to talk about
the situation. Like many other residents, he didn't think that the
mayor's plan to tear down and rebuild the Courts as a mix of high-
end and public housing apartments was motivated by the city's
concern for College Hill Courts residents. He thought it was an
excuse to tear down his home so that the now glitzy downtown
waterfront could colonize the land in the Westside.

"He was worried that he'd been living out there all those years,
and then they want to rip apart the people and the place they live
at," said Hettie. "He said, 'Momma, these are our homes. Why
should we give up our homes just to run a Riverport and them
condominiums over there?'"

Even more than his sense of fairness, Michael was thinking
about his independence. He'd already watched a handful of the
city's public housing projects, including his former home, Harriet
Tubman, disappear. He doubted that he'd be able to find another
place to live on his own if the city closed College Hill Courts, too.
He was a grown man now, and he couldn't imagine moving back
home.

"I am not—I will not go back to live with my mom," explained
Hutchins. "What will I look like, a grown man, at home with his
momma? At forty, at that!" he said. "I got to have my own roof over
my head—that's where it starts with."

Michael Hutchins leads the march to protect College Hill Courts and demand affordable housing for Chattanooga, Tennessee. Photo by Jared Story.

Other residents without the safety net of having a mother's home to move back to were even more scared. One mother couldn't stop crying when she heard the news. Another woman, Beulah Washington, declared she would fight as hard as her sixty-seven-year-old body could stand. She'd moved to the Westside when her former apartment in McCallie Homes was converted into a new mixed-income development, and this would be her second public housing displacement.[147]

The city didn't hear about these concerns at the first meeting it held on Purpose Built, because the residents weren't invited. Instead, the crowd consisted of approximately fifty of the city's elected officials and business leaders, who listened attentively to Purpose Built's presentation. The reception was positive. Funded by Warren Buffett, former hedge director Julian Robertson, and Atlanta developer Tom Cousins, Purpose Built describes its mission as to "transform struggling neighborhoods into vibrant and sustainable communities where everyone has the opportunity to thrive."[148] It specializes in redeveloping public housing complexes, and its development projects have a well-quantified track record of decreasing crime and bringing businesses like grocery stores and YMCAs into impoverished neighborhoods, such as in the East Lake community of Atlanta.

The secret to Purpose Built's success is that it changes these neighborhoods by displacing the majority of the communities' residents and building beautiful facilities that attract families who can afford higher rent. The group doesn't calculate whether it turns around the lives of the former residents who have been forced out of their homes and flung into the far corners of the for-profit housing market without any type of support. At the December meeting, the mayor indicated that he had his eye on a few sites for Purpose Built's program, including College Hill Courts.

One of the three Westside residents allowed at the meeting was Roxann Larson, the resident council president of Dogwood Manor, a Chattanooga Housing Authority-managed apartment tower in the Westside reserved for low-income seniors. She was also one of the few in attendance who wasn't impressed with the plan.

"I fear that the high-rise buildings will be turned into condos which will displace all the people in the building," Larson told the *Chattanooga Times Free Press* after the meeting. "They paint a rosy picture but, in reality, when the move people out, they can't afford to move back."[149]

Michael first heard about Purpose Built when Ash-Lee Henderson, a volunteer with Chattanooga Organizing for Action, knocked on his door. A grassroots social justice group that began in the summer of 2010, Chattanooga Organizing for Action focuses on training people in low-income and minority neighborhoods to become community leaders. It operates outside the government grant system that often hamstrings nonprofits, and many of its members have a more radical analysis about what type of future they'd like to see.

One Chattanooga Organizing for Action member, Landon Howard, explained that what drew him to join the group was that he thought the country's underlying economic structure was so unequal, he no longer believed he could help people from within that system.

"I went to school for social work, but the more I saw what was happening around me, the idea of the welfare state shattered," he said. "The economic and political systems are collapsing at the same time, and people are starting to see other options."

Michael already knew about Chattanooga Organizing for Action and a little about activism as well. On a Saturday afternoon six months earlier, he had looked out his window to see more than one hundred people gathered on the street outside his apartment. Michael rushed down to join the sign-waving crowd. He learned that Chattanooga Organizing for Action was working with residents to demand that a new grocery come to the Westside. The area's only food store, Dollar General, had closed, forcing Michael and the rest of the residents to walk a full three miles to shop at the nearest supermarket. The bus system was unreliable, and few owned cars or could afford the $20 taxi ride. Elected officials had merely shrugged their shoulders when a fifteen-year-old Westside resident complained in an op-ed in the *Chattanooga Times Free Press*. The city had no control over where the free-market chose to set up shop, they argued, apparently forgetting about the hundreds of millions of dollars in incentives that the city had recently funneled to developers to convince them to build downtown. Chattanooga Organizing for Action, on the other hand, read the op-ed and began planning the march.

Michael's first day of activism was exhilarating.

"People were honking and cheering as we marched up MLK Drive," he said. The next day, he even saw his picture in the newspaper—the first time in his life that his face had been printed for others to see. The campaign was successful, too; a year and a half later, a supermarket named One Stop Shop opened across the street from College Hill Courts.

Ash-Lee Henderson invited Michael to come to the Westside Community Association's meetings, held at the Renaissance Presbyterian Church right up the street from his apartment. He began attending the gatherings and even joined the group at one of the City Council Housing Committee meetings at the end of

January. He thought he'd be able to voice his opposition to the plan at the committee meeting, but the councilwoman told the residents—much to their anger—that they wouldn't be able to speak at all. Michael was dismayed. First the mayor didn't invite Westside residents to the Purpose Built presentation, and now residents were barred from sharing their opinions with the city council. Michael felt that the city didn't care at all what he thought about his own home.

The next week, Michael joined the Westside Community Association and Chattanooga Organizing for Action as they launched the campaign "NOT for Sale!," which demanded that the city not sell off College Hill Courts and displace any more public housing residents. At the press conference to announce the campaign, Michael stood rigidly, his jaw tightened and his hands shoved into his sweatshirt pockets to keep his right arm from shaking. Even though Michael was shy and spoke only a few words that day, the new campaign kicked off a whirlwind of interviews, cameras, and press conferences. Michael began to emerge as a voice of the community.

"It was a wild ride, and that's when I needed to join," said Michael. "This is affecting me, so I knew I needed to speak up."

The mix of residents and community members working on "NOT for Sale!" were an eclectic group. Gloria Griffin and Reverend Leroy Griffith, two prominent civil rights activists who lived in the Westside, saw the fight for College Hill Courts as a continuation of the racial justice movement. One of them often ran meetings while the other nitpicked, scolded, and sprinkled the conversation with stories, which included bricks flying through their home's window (the two were one of the first interracial marriages in the state) and FBI inquiries. Other

Westside residents included Carl Epperson, a former candidate for mayor who scooted down the hill to the meetings in an electric wheelchair, ferrying his dog on his lap; Karl Kenrick, an elderly man with a prominent comb-over; and Beulah Washington, the woman who had pledged to fight with whatever her sixty-seven-year-old body had left. Roxann Larson, whose organizing at her public housing site up the hill had helped rid the high-rise of bed bugs, joined the fight for College Hill Courts, along with Adair Darland, who went before the City Council on Valentine's Day to ask that the city save her home rather than break her heart. Younger activists such as Landon Howard, Perrin Lance, and Ash-Lee Henderson came from Chattanooga Organizing for Action; they saw the fight for the Westside as part of a much longer struggle to stop the government from dispossessing and displacing people of color from their land. Chattanooga was one of the first points on the Trail of Tears, thus its founding was based on the mass removal of the Cherokee Nation. Later, in the 1950s, the city seized large swaths of land owned by African Americans, razing the homes and businesses to build the very highways that curve around the Westside and cut it off from the rest of the city.

In 2011, as Occupy spread across the country, the group adopted the movement's meeting style, complete with the "up-twinkle" hand signals, a facilitator to ensure that the meetings ran smoothly, and a consensus-based decision-making process. Michael became the group's timekeeper, diligently making sure that no one spoke past the limit. He took the job seriously, and he sometimes slammed his hand on the table when people rambled. He also joined Chattanooga Organizing for Action's weekly leadership classes for organizers.

Perrin Lance noticed that Michael had a strong speaking

presence, even though he was reserved and still sometimes fumbled for basic words. One day Lance pulled him aside and suggested that Michael take on a leadership role in the campaign, speaking to his neighbors and about what was going on and trying to convince them to defend College Hill Courts. Michael thought seriously about the idea. He spoke about it with his mother, who remembers that Lance's words made a strong impression on her son.

Michael liked the idea of being someone that people might look up to, she recalled. He'd read so many negative things about the people who lived in College Hill Courts, and those words bothered him, even though he didn't believe them to be true.

"I think I'm a pretty good person," he once said. But he spoke the words as if he'd really been forced to consider whether he was or not.

Hettie liked the idea, too.

"This might be your calling in life," she told her son. Although it looked unlikely that Michael and a dozen other Westside residents and organizers would be able to thwart a city plan backed by the business community, she had faith.

"People in numbers work magic," she told him. "In great big numbers, they work magic."

Michael replied, "I'm going to fight. And if we lose, we lose. But I'm going to try."

Michael and the Westside Community Association embarked on a mission to bring together the city's public housing residents and supportive community members under a series of demands. They created a petition demanding that the city replace all the public housing units it has destroyed in the last decade; rebuild public housing apartments on a one-to-one replacement rate thereafter; and require new developments to include low-income units.

At the end of February 2012, Mayor Ron Littlefield held another meeting with Purpose Built representatives. He was still quite keen on Purpose Built transforming the Westside. The city government seemed stuck; the Chattanooga Housing Authority commanded little more than $3 million annually and estimated it needed more than $50 million to make the necessary renovations to College Hill Courts. Skeptical organizers, meanwhile, called this estimate "death by numbers."

At the February meeting, Westside residents were once again promised they could speak, but Michael was abruptly cut off.

"Who will ask the questions if I don't?" Michael asked later. "I may be taking up the time but I'm trying to get my point across. The last question I was going to ask was: 'What if Purpose Built came to your neighborhood?' But that's when I got cut off."

Michael started to get noticed in his community. Some people didn't like what he was doing; they wanted to get out of College Hill Courts, and they believed that the Section 8 vouchers would be a better bet. But others were glad someone from College Hill Courts was speaking up about the fears that so many harbored. Sometimes he received praise from other residents as he walked down the street. Once Howard Akins, Michael's uncle, who had first inspired him to start running, rose to his feet to applaud Michael. Akins had just seen one of Michael's TV segments and he was proud to see what his nephew had become.

By the beginning of April, more than 1,200 people had signed the petition. The Westside Community Association decided it was time to present the document to City Council and force the elected officials to finally listen to their demands. On April 3, Michael, the rest of the Westside Community Association and more than one hundred other residents and supporters marched from Renaissance Church to the City Council building downtown. Gloria Griffin carried a sign reading THE WESTSIDE SHALL NOT BE MOVED. Other signs asked, WHOSE PURPOSE? and declared YOUR PROFIT MARGINS CAUSED HOMELESSNESS. Passing pedestrians clapped. The marchers sang the civil rights song "Ain't Gonna Let Nobody Turn Me 'Round," the same tune the Freedom Riders sang in 1961 when their journey to desegregate the South landed them in the Parchman Penitentiary in Mississippi.[150]

As Michael walked in, he was nervous. Inside the City Council Building, Michael was one of only three people who were going to address the city council and present the petition.

"It was a lot of people; it was more people than I expected. I was nervous. Period," said Michael later. This day wasn't the first time he'd spoken in public, but it was the first time he was charged with presenting the demands of more than one thousand people to the city's elected officials.

The energy inside the elegant wood-paneled room felt electric. The march had made an impression on the crowd. Roxann Larson later described the event, saying, "I just got the chills and wanted to cry, I was so proud to be a part of that day."

Michael approached the podium. He and Perrin had written his speech together, which Michael had secured in a blue folder that he clutched throughout the march.

"My name is Michael Hutchins," he began, his eyes trained on the paper, his voice loud and deliberate. He had practiced; he hoped his brain wouldn't mess up his words. "I reside at 742 West Twelfth Street at College Hill Courts in the Westside. I am here presenting thousands of signatures on a petition demanding that city government—that the city government make the right to housing a priority. As you know, housing for poor people, working people, and people of color is in crisis.

"Thousands of people sit on— on the closed waiting lists for public and low-income housing. In the past decade, six public housing communities have been demolished, and now my home, College Hill, is being talked about as next. Over four thousand people are homeless every year in Chattanooga, and a big cause of that is eviction. That's the threat we face as public housing residents.

"We cannot continue to live in this oppression. That's why we've given you three proposals to consider. First, for every unit of public housing torn down, another one must be built. Second, we want a one-for-one replacement of all housing—of all public housing units torn down in the last ten years. Last, all new housing developments in the city must include some low-income units."

He began to speak faster and a little more comfortably. The next paragraphs were the ones that he'd written on his own.

"For public housing and low-income residents, there are few places left for us to go. I feel like our homes are under attack and that the people who want to destroy our communities are right on our doorsteps. We need a better plan for housing in Chattanooga. We need you to—we need you to stand up." He swept his left arm in the air, gesturing at the row of city council members sitting behind their raised bench to his right. "You being the city council, and work with us. We need elected leaders to have our back."

"So far we have been shut out of the process. Meetings have been held without our knowledge, groups like Purpose Built Communities have been invited *not* by us. They have held meetings we all weren't invited to, and when the meetings were held, I wanted to speak up for my people, but I wasn't allowed to. Even though that moment made me feel low, we have made up for that silence by the voices of everyone here today.

"In closing, I want to see results. I want our right to housing defended. The people of public and low-income housing are organizing to protect our homes. Chattanooga supports the right to housing, we ask that you do the same."

He looked up as he said the last line: "Thank you for allowing me to voice my opinion on this matter."

The room filled with applause, although it was quieter than it might have been because many listeners involved with Occupy expressed their approval by raising their fingers and twinkling them in the air. Months later, Michael still smiles when he remembers the speech, even though he's quick to point out that he messed up a few times.

Two months after Michael presented the signatures to City Council, the *Chattanooga Times Free Press* reported that the plans for Purpose Built had gone from "full boil to back burner." In the face of the opposition, the Chattanooga Housing Authority had quickly distanced itself from Mayor Littlefield's plan. CHA executive director Betsy McCright said that instead of pushing Purpose Built she planned to organize a visioning team, which would include residents, the following year to strategize what to do about College Hill. The mayor's talks with Purpose Built ceased after the City Council speech, although he remained adamant that something would happen to College Hill sooner or later.

"It will be replaced at some time in the future. What we have tried to impress on the people living there is that we intend the best for them," Mayor Littlefield said.

Meanwhile, the Westside Community Association was making its own plans. Throughout the spring and summer, it drafted an alternative proposal to demolition and privatization: a community revitalization program to renovate the buildings through volunteer work days. Under the plan, construction companies would donate the materials, and residents and local unions would perform the manual labor. Mayor Littlefield said the plan was "completely unrealistic."

To residents and activists, however, the plan offered an opportunity to show how a community that is empowered to make decisions about its future can control and manage land. Whether the plan is feasible will likely never be tested, since both Mayor Littlefield and CHA director McCright dismissed the plan outright.

Michael, however, thought it was an incredible idea.

"That would be awesome, so awesome," he said. "At least we're trying. You can't fault nobody for that."

Michael knew that even though he and the group defeated Purpose Built, College Hill Courts were still marked for demolition. He stepped back from the Westside Community Association after the flurry of work during the spring of 2012, but he remains ready to resume organizing if and when the city once again threatens him with displacement. He is proud that he and other residents spoke up, and he is pleased that the media exposure inspired the rest of the city to stop criticizing public housing from afar and instead rally behind the projects' benefits. Most of all, Michael is happy that, finally, the community saw and heard his full potential.

"For the people who never see you, they can get a conception about you," he explained. "Now at least they'll get a voice to go with that picture."

Voices, he learned, have a way of carrying further than legs could ever go.

Jimmya, 10 (left), plays cards with her sister, Justice, 8 (right), on the porch of the family's reclaimed house.
Photo by Brent Lewis.

LIBERATED

Martha Biggs and Jajuanna Walker
Chicago, Illinois

Her mother was here! Jajuanna rushed to greet Martha, who had come to visit her oldest daughter. It was June 17, 2011, and Jajuanna had just graduated middle school. She'd been living with her father since the threat of intervention by the Department of Children and Social Services forced Martha to split the kids up. But today, her mother was here—and she came with a surprise.

"We got a home," Jajuanna remembers Martha telling her. The information didn't immediately register.

"What? We got a home?" Jajuanna asked.

"Yeah, we got a home," Martha repeated in her typical straightforward manner. "You wanna come see it?"

There was, indeed, a house: a 101-year-old two-family home built with red bricks. It had a front porch, a backyard, and a pretty second-floor balcony supported by pillars and ringed by a short wrought-iron railing. It looked like a lot of the neighboring houses on South Prairie Avenue about a block from where Interstate 90 cuts diagonally through the South Side of Chicago. Inside, the house was clean and simple, with newly polished hardwood floors and freshly painted caramel-colored walls.

The house hadn't always looked this way. When Martha first visited it, the day after Patricia Hill handed her the keys, it was a typical vacant house in the neighborhood. Deutsche Bank claimed to own it and had foreclosed on the owner, Patricia's daughter Stacy, in 2009. The bank, however, failed to assume ownership because its own law firm reported that the foreclosure documents had been altered or fabricated.[151] In the spring of 2011, while Martha was sleeping in a car, the court halted Hill's foreclosure proceeding, as well as nearly two thousand others. As the house sat vacant, strippers tore out the toilet, the copper wiring, the pipes, the radiator, the ceiling fans and almost everything in the kitchen, including some cabinet doors. When Martha first entered, there were holes in the walls and trash on the floor. Still, it hadn't been taken over by a gang; it hadn't been set on fire; and it hadn't been flooded. It was salvageable. Martha parked her white minivan in front of the house and began to work.

But what was more astonishing than the house was the scene in the front yard. As Jajuanna watched, people carrying signs and reporters shouldering heavy news cameras descended on the front lawn. Channel 2 arrived, and Channel 7, and Fox, and even a reporter from the New York Times. The grass was covered in posters reading RECLAIMED BY THE COMMUNITY and STOP FORECLOSURE! Members of the Chicago Anti-Eviction Campaign arrived clad in the group's black T-shirts. Reporters set up a podium of microphones.

The Biggs family had lived in plenty of foreclosed houses over the last decade. But this was something different. This was not just a house. It was a stage.

The crowd began shouting, "Fight! Fight! Fight! 'Cause Housing Is a Human Right!" Justice, Jimmya, and Davion took up the chant with their sing-song voices as they played tag on the front porch.

Suddenly, all eyes were on Martha and her children.

"Martha! Martha! Martha!" the crowd chanted as she stepped up to the microphones. After years of silence and invisibility, the Biggs women finally had their audience.

"Hello. My name is Martha Biggs, and I'm from Cabrini

Green," Martha began. She clutched Justice's head to her waist, and her daughter shyly buried her face in Martha's side. Jajuanna and Jimmya stood behind their mother's right shoulder. Jajuanna was almost as tall as Martha, and with her hair swept back and her face set, she looked older than her fifteen years.

"I've been there since I was like two years old," continued Martha. "I was evicted. Homeless. On the street. Nowhere to go. Got a job. Worked hard to support my kids. Was homeless again because the building I moved into was in foreclosure. So therefore me and my family had to take another journey to be homeless again. To sleep in our cars. To go to different units, different family members' houses. To run around. No place to go."

The crowd was silent except for the snapping of the reporters' cameras.

"We came up with a conclusion not to give up. Always fight. Never sit down. Keep it moving. Keep it working. This is what happens when you never sit down. This is what you accomplish— stuff like this here."

Martha continued.

"It's for the future of my kids. They ain't got to worry about where they going to sleep. Where they going to go to wash up at. Or where their next pair of shoes or socks going to get cleaned at. They ain't got to worry about that anymore. They ain't got to worry about any of those things because I never gave up, never stopped trying," she said.

Then, surrounded by her kids and captured on television, Martha declared the house liberated.

The idea of home liberation is simple. Currently, there are millions of vacant, bank-owned houses across the country dragging down property values, bankrupting cities, fueling crime and creating an almost irreconcilable rupture in the theory of supply and demand.

In well-off suburban areas, these vacant houses are symbols of the United States' seemingly limitless ability to produce excess. In poorer areas like the South Side of Chicago, they symbolize a darker characteristic of America's capitalist business culture: the ability to allow those with staggering excess to coexist alongside, and prey upon, those in desperate need.

As the houses sit vacant, there are millions of Americans, like the Biggses, who have nowhere to live and fight through life each day as capitalism's refugees. Some were evicted from their homes through foreclosure; others didn't even have the luxury of owning a detached house to begin with. What they share is a desire to survive through conditions so difficult that getting through each day should be celebrated as a triumph of will. But unlike the vacant houses, these people are not symbols; they are our neighbors, friends, family members, and classmates. And they have had enough of living as refugees—or perhaps exiles—in their own country simply because they can't afford the price of a place to call home.

Martha's was the first publicized home liberation in Chicago and one of the first in the country since the economic collapse began. Nearly everyone from the land reclamation movement was there. It was an emotional day for organizers, who rarely saw home liberations actually happen—especially in such a public manner. Rob Robinson of the New York City chapter of a group called Take Back the Land remembers watching Justice run out of the house with a piece of plywood on which she'd scrawled in her eight-year-old handwriting: THANK YOU EVERYONE.

"I just started to tear up," Robinson recalls. "J.R. was talking to me and I was like, 'Not now J.R., I need a minute.'"

For Martha's children, the day was something they'd only dreamed of.

"I never thought we'd be here," said Jajuanna.

Home liberation as a political movement has existed in the United States since as early as the late 1960s in New York City. Groups like the Young Lords and Harlem Fight Back began organizing building takeovers both as a strategy to solve growing homelessness and as a protest against the city's practice of intentionally keeping thousands of apartment buildings vacant until housing prices rose. The movement's days of coordinated takeovers are legendary. In 1979, teams of people reclaimed thirty buildings for immediate use in Harlem, East New York, and Newark, New Jersey, all in the same weekend. In the 1980s, people liberated another thirty apartment buildings across the Lower East Side and as many vacant lots, which they turned into community gardens.

The city waged pitched battles over the occupied buildings. Frank Morales, a priest involved in home liberation in the Lower East Side, remembers how hundreds of riot cops wielding automatic rifles used to surround the buildings, which Morales and his comrades barricaded shut.

"One night, they brought a wrecking ball at midnight into one of the houses I was living in," remembers Morales. "I lived on the top floor—it was a six-floor tenement—and they knocked the front wall down so my room was exposed. I just looked at this wrecking ball swinging towards me. I managed to run out with two bags of my belongings."

After more than a decade of struggle, the city finally handed over titles to several of the buildings, which remain occupied today.

The movement resurged in October 2006, when a group called Take Back the Land seized a vacant public lot in Miami and created an encampment called the Umoja Village, which housed more than fifty people for six months. An African American-led group, Take Back the Land argues that the relationship to land lies at the root of racial and economic inequalities in the United States. The group envisions a new system in which land use is controlled by the community and housing is enshrined as a human right. As the foreclosure crisis worsened, Take Back the Land grew into a national network that works with displaced families to liberate bank-owned houses such as Martha Biggs's. Since 2006, Take Back the Land and other housing groups have helped communities take over dozens of vacant, bank-owned homes in Miami, Madison, Rochester, Detroit, New York City, Chicago, Los Angeles, and other cities. The ever growing need for shelter fuels the movement. But there's also a moral question, grounded in human rights, evoked by the coexistence of millions of empty bank-owned houses and millions of families who need a place to live. Maybe homes, these groups reason, shouldn't be considered commodities at all.

"We are in a transformative moment," said Max Rameau, one of the leaders of Take Back the Land. "I think we're going to have significant changes in the way people think about not just housing but land itself."

Rameau and others have turned the ongoing foreclosure crisis into a window of opportunity to challenge the current conception of individualistic, profit-fueled land ownership. The group is creating community land trusts, which allow neighborhoods to make decisions about how homes and land are used. Their goal: to liberate thousands of properties from bank control and to place those properties in community land trusts that would protect them from being used as commodities. Ultimately, the move to take homes off the market is not just a housing movement. It is also a push to de-commodify society, to begin to articulate a world in which monetary transactions no longer control the value and identity of human lives.

In the years since Martha's home liberation she has grown into one of the most prominent housing organizers in the country. She often speaks at conferences in New York City, Miami and New Orleans, and she helps J.R. lead the Anti-Eviction Campaign meetings. Most significantly, home liberations are sweeping Chicago, and many people give Martha credit for catalyzing the movement.

"Martha kicked this all off," said John Newman, who now works full time to liberate and repair houses across the South Side of Chicago.

Multiple autonomous groups, including the Chicago Anti-Eviction Campaign, Take Back the Land, and Occupy Homes Chicago, compete to see which can liberate more homes from bank control. Like Martha, the majority of organizers are themselves currently or formerly people without a stable place to live. It is a decidedly low-budget affair. For a while, one man pawned his own belongings to buy locks and construction supplies to rehabilitate houses for other people. The priority is to house families, particularly single women with children, who often do the majority of the clean-up work themselves.

Erica Johnson, for example, moved into a liberated home on the far South Side with help from members of Occupy Homes Chicago. The first day she and her kids visited the house, it was filled with garbage and drug paraphernalia. It lacked electricity and indoor plumbing. The front yard was overrun with waist-high weeds. But when her ride came to take the family back to the shelter where they lived, Johnson's fifteen-year-old daughter said they should stay and live there while they fixed it up. The next day, Johnson began whacking the weeds with a big knife. Within a few weeks, the inside of the house was clean, and Johnson was working with her neighbor to fix the plumbing.

Martha Biggs's daughter, Justice, 8, stands outside her family's liberated home. Martha Biggs chose the name Justice for her daughter meaning, "It's justice that I will never be homeless again." Photo by Brent Lewis.

In this sense, what Martha, J.R., and the rest are building is not a social service agency that shelters families. She and others are creating a new economic structure in which the rules are simple: meet people's basic needs and employ everyone.

Martha's favorite case study is her friend Thomas Turner. When he first started working with Martha and Occupy Chicago, he had no place to live and was more than a little mentally unstable. He sometimes relapsed into the drug addiction that had kept him cycling in and out of prison for years. Frankly, no one wanted Turner around. He embodied the failures of Chicago, where the current system keeps nearly 20 percent of the residents in minority neighborhoods out of work and brands more than half of the African American men felons for life.

"But did you ever think Thomas was crazy because he don't have a place to go?" asked Martha. "That when you go home at night, sit down at your table eating dinner, he doesn't have a table or a dinner? That he's outside? And that that might drive a man crazy?"

In the spring of 2012, Turner took over a bank-owned house and began fixing it up. Everything changed. He stood straighter, and he stopped using drugs. He took another house, and then a third and a fourth, fixing them up for others. When a local property owner saw what he was doing, she donated three more. Lawyers reached out to him, and soon Turner founded his own nonprofit. He appointed a board of directors and began doing radio interviews.

"This is about making our own economic system," said Turner as he showed me around one of the homes he'd renovated. The walls were freshly painted and decorated with intricate stenciling of birds. In the other room, a young couple that Turner was mentoring moved buckets of paint and mop water. The two were barely in their twenties, and neither had a stable home, so Turner was teaching them how to secure and renovate foreclosed houses, with the hope that they'd take one for themselves soon.

"I'm trying to build a system where homeless people have jobs, where we can employ them," said Turner. "I don't have all the answers, but I do know that housing is a human right,"

This idea that all people have the right to a safe and decent place to live is one that, for an increasing number of Americans, overrides issues of profit margins, interest rates, or even property contracts. It's a vision that Martha has harbored for decades, ever since her own overcrowded youth in Cabrini Green. But no matter how rapidly this movement grows in Chicago, Martha never forgets to focus on her and her children's own home.

One sweltering summer afternoon, Martha and her kids gathered in the living room, turned on the Nintendo Wii and did what families should only do behind closed doors: competitively danced to Michael Jackson.

"Go Justice!" Martha yelled as the nine-year-old competed against John Newman, another housing activist who has been living with the family. "Thriller" blared from the television. Beads of sweat dripped off Newman's forehead. He was a smoother dancer than Justice, but the girl was bolder.

Two other activists arrived. There was work to be done; the four had plans to go clean up a foreclosed house. But for a few moments, Martha decided to enjoy what she'd been searching for in her quest for home over the past decade—family time.

Justice flung her body through the stomping pivots, but she was no match for Newman. So Martha challenged her friend, thinking to avenge her daughter's defeat. The song began, and Martha fixed her eyes on the screen and whispered the words as she danced.

"Who gave you the right to shake my family? And who gave you the right to shake my baby—she needs me," she said.

Martha kept her body high, while Newman crouched down, stuck out his tongue, and smiled so hard the corners of his eyes crinkled. He had far more points than she did, but Martha kept threatening that she was getting her second wind. Both had sweat pouring down their necks; it was the hottest day of the summer's worst heat wave. Davion ran into the room and rolled his weight onto his tippy toes, gave a quick shoulder shimmy, and ran back out. Justice sat on Jimmya's lap and waved her arms in time with the music.

Newman won again. He was unstoppable. Martha pulled up her T-shirt and leaned over the box fan to cool off. Jajuanna stepped into the center of the living room, gave her mother a high five and goaded Newman into one last dance. He was exhausted, but agreed. Like her mother, Jajuanna executed the moves mechanically. Newman was probably a better dancer, but he was so tired that Jajuanna won. The girl jumped up and down in celebration.

"I'm going to help you pick your face up off the floor!" she cried. It was her favorite phrase that summer, and everyone in the room laughed.

When the team finally left the house to work, still covered in sweat, Newman remarked: "We're taking over homes so we can do that."

Martha Biggs's new home isn't perfect. Her kids, especially Jimmya, are still worried that they might be evicted. Martha is already making preparations just in case they have to move. Nothing is ever permanent, especially in activism. But ultimately, the success of a home liberation—and of all social movements, really—is creating a new chapter to a story that everyone said was outside your control.

After the Biggs family moved into their new house, Martha asked each of her kids to write a letter to publish in the local newspaper. Jajuanna sat down and wrote hers by hand. She was too shy to publish it at the time, but she held on to the piece of paper and shared it years later.

THE STORY OF MY LIFE

by Jajuanna Walker

I was born and raised in Cabrini Green. When we thought we had it good and moved on the West Side in a house that had been in foreclosed without our knowing it. And when I ran away that did not help the problem any more it made it worse because my mom had to take off work to come find me and she lost her job because of me. And after that we got kicked out of our house and we were homeless again and had no place to live or stay for that matter. But we had the type of family that we could lean on sometimes but in this case we could. They let us stay at their house because we had no place to go. But in our minds we knew we could not stay forever. So there were times we didn't go to our family's house and slept in our car. It may not have been comfortable but we knew there was no other choice. And at one point through all this I hurt myself because I hated what we were going through and I just wanted it to stop. But as I got help I learned to deal with my problems and that was not the smartest way to do it. But the real way to deal with my problems is to talk it out or write it down. And I got help and I talked my way out of a depression. But when I did try to kill myself they called DCFS [Department of Child and Family Services]. But now I am 100 percent strong after coming from my dad's house for about a month or so and I have not thought about killing myself since then. But back to me and my family, even though we were homeless my mom made sure we had a meal every night. But at one point we had to separate

158

because someone called DCFS [Department of Child and Family Services] and told them we were sleeping in our car and at that point it gave my mom the time she needed to get us a place to stay. When we were separated we really didn't get to see each other at all not even at school. But when my mom got her things together and did what she needed to do she finally got what she always wanted. She got a place to call home and the family back together. But there is still a struggle of keeping the house. But the best thing is that we are all back together in a place we call home.

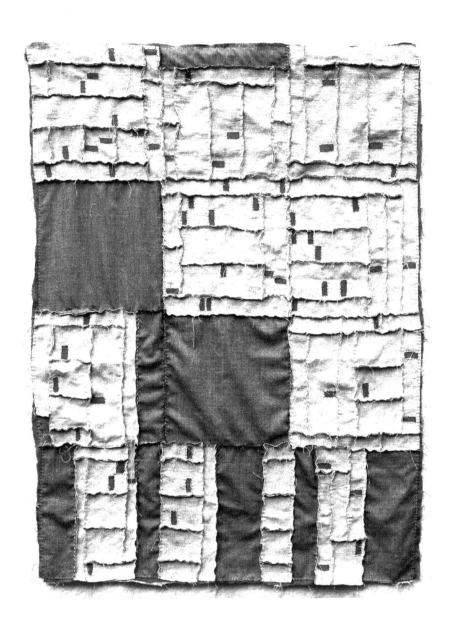

Foreclosure quilt representing Albuquerque, New Mexico, by Kathryn Clark, 2012. Made from linen, wool, yarn and embroidery thread; 35" x 47". Foreclosures in small dark-stitched rectangles.

EPILOGUE

My daughter and her husband lost their house the other day. Yeah, right. We're on track. . . .[152]

—AN ANONYMOUS COMMENTER ON REUTERS ONLINE

Today, the United States is said to be experiencing a housing recovery. The financial press frequently pronounces that this economic rebound is "on track" and the "housing market has finally turned the corner."[153] But these projections have almost nothing to do with the vast majority of the nation. Rising home values are little consolation for the ten million people who have lost the places that they called home—and the millions more who are still threatened with eviction or foreclosure. Rising rental prices make it still more difficult for the displaced to find somewhere else to live. As for the broader economic recovery, in 2010 the top 1 percent of Americans captured a staggering 93 percent of the nation's income gains.[154] Economists predict that this sharply uneven "recovery" will continue.

Black families have already lost more than half their median wealth since the economic crisis began. One *Washington Post* article warns, "The implosion of the subprime lending market has left a scar on the finances of black Americans—one that not only has wiped out a generation of economic progress but could leave them at a financial disadvantage for decades."[155] For all Americans, economists predict it could take the next twenty years to recover the amount of money lost between 2005 and 2010 in the housing market alone.[156]

No banker, lawyer, or Wall Street executive has gone to prison for the industry's widespread illegal practices—not to mention for crashing the global economy. The lack of prosecution is widely regarded as a moral hazard, one that encourages bankers to continue flouting legislation and regulation, because there is no threat of punishment. Ironically, many deployed the moral hazard argument early in the foreclosure crisis as a justification for not reducing victimized families' mortgage principals, with the rationale that these families and their neighbors wouldn't learn the lesson of financial responsibility unless millions were evicted from their homes. The absence of criminal consequences even inspired a PBS investigative documentary titled *The Untouchables*—a reference both to the bankers' privileged legal status and to the lowest caste in India, a class of people who are viewed as so impure and despicable that others literally do not want to have physical contact with them.

In January 2013, ten Wall Street banks paid, collectively, $8.5 billion to silence a review process of millions of mortgage documents that would have further illuminated the industry's fraudulent practices. That same week, the Consumer Financial Protection Bureau outlined regulations for mortgage pushers that included "a legal shield for banks [that] would largely insulate banks from lawsuits."[157] Mortgage pushers "applauded the new regulations."[158] Meanwhile, box stores like WalMart and Costco began packaging and selling a big new product: home mortgages.

This is all to say that the housing situation for Americans of all races and ethnicities has only grown worse as the so-called economic recovery has progressed. What has changed, albeit slowly, is the *idea* of home and housing. Like Griggs Wimbley, Bertha Garrett, Michael Hutchins, and Martha Biggs, more and more Americans are arguing that housing should be a right, not a privilege, in the United States. In 2008, in an unprecedented move, the United Nations rapporteur on the right to adequate housing made an official trip to the United States, where she toured seven cities and met with hundreds of residents who testified that the nation's exclusive, for-profit housing system violates the internationally recognized Universal Declaration of Human Rights. The following year, the majority of Americans surveyed supported a nationwide suspension of foreclosures.[159] In 2010, Take Back the Land organized a national month of live-in actions "in the spirit of the civil rights movement." By 2011, housing activism was sweeping all major cities. Communities had orchestrated dozens of home takeovers and hundreds of eviction blockades across the country since the housing crisis had begun. In Boston, the longtime housing justice group City Life/Vida Urbana had organized twenty-six successful eviction blockades. In Detroit, community members had taken over and rehabbed nearly an entire block of homes and declared them liberated of market value.

When researcher and urban planner Chester Hartman published *The Case for A Right to Housing* in 1998, he conceded that the idea that "housing is a human right" could be regarded as "futile, quixotic, even bizarre."[160] Today, the words are inked onto cardboard signs and paraded through the streets in dozens of cities and small towns. They are painted on banners and hung on homes where owners resisted eviction or community members took over vacant, bank-owned houses. And the principle is slowly being put into practice. In Rochester, New York, Take Back the Land has established a community land trust where de-commoditized homes can be communally controlled by the neighborhood.

As the climate justice movement exploded onto the global stage in late 2012, catalyzed by the indigenous people–led Idle No More protests and the shock of Hurricane Sandy, the importance of the housing movement became even more evident. The capitalist economic system of privileging banks over homeowners threatens society with miseries far greater than predatory loans, foreclosure abuse, and mass evictions. It also threatens the sustainability of civilization itself by profiting from war and environmentally destructive practices that accelerate climate destabilization and threaten the balance of life on Earth.

This story began with the history of how the United States' model of property and individual ownership has rendered it an inhospitable land for generations of African Americans and other people of color. It ends with the prospect of an Earth that could become uninhabitable for all. But the heroes of the story are the people in the middle, those like Griggs, Bertha, Michael, Martha and millions of others who refuse to have their dreams foreclosed, people who fight not only to save their own homes, but to create a more just and sustainable system for everyone. Their struggle is ours. And for the sake of all of us, it is one that we must win.

ACKNOWLEDGEMENTS

This project wouldn't have been possible without hundreds of people.

Martha Biggs, Griggs Wimbley, Michael Hutchins, and Bertha Garrett, thank you for welcoming me into your homes and sharing your stories with me. I hope you will consider this book a celebration of your courage. To all the organizers and resisters across the country, thank you for inspiring me and others to work for a more just system. A special thanks to Rob Robinson, Max Rameau and Anthony Newby for guiding me through this project with patience and generosity.

Greg Ruggiero and Joe Nevins, thank you for inviting me to become part of Zuccotti Park Press and for the months of editing and visioning. Nathan Schneider, thank you for being a role model of an activist-journalist and for editing my articles on housing activism. Fred Strebeigh and Anne Fadiman, thank you for inspiring me to write narrative nonfiction and for showing me the power of storytelling. Jim Connolly, thank you for teaching me how to write to begin with, and for encouraging me to pursue this passion throughout my life.

My own housing was fairly precarious throughout the course of this year-long project. Thank you everyone who housed me and gave me a place to write, including: Stephanie Richards in Durham; Landon Howard and Mary-Bricker Jenkins in Chattanooga; Alejandra and David Cruz, Bobby Hull, T.K., Anthony Newby, and

Monique White in Minneapolis; Martha Biggs, David Williams, Loren Taylor, and Ed Voci in Chicago; the residents of the Riverdale Mobile Home Park in Jersey Shore, Pennsylvania; Jim Novick and Nicole Hagner in New Jersey; Greg Chase in Cheshire, Connecticut; and Nathaniel Obler and Katherine Mullan in New York City. A special thanks to Cynthia Santos and Juan Carlos Ruiz in New York City, for providing both a home and a very close friendship.

Lastly, Diego Ibañez, thank you for the hours of editing and the endless conversations. *Y más que todo, gracias por tu amor.*

NOTES

1   Martin Luther King Jr., *Where Do We Go From Here: Chaos or Community?* (New York: Harper & Row, 1967), p. 118.
2   Jeannette Wicks-Lim, "The Great Recession in Black Wealth," *Dollars & Sense*, www.dollarsandsense.org/archives/2012/0112wicks-lim.html, accessed April 2013.
3   Ibid.
4   Ibid.
5   Tami Luhby, "Worsening wealth inequality by race," *CNNMoney*, June 21, 2012, http://money.cnn.com/2012/06/21/news/economy/wealth-gap-race/index.htm, accessed April 2013.
6   The Universal Declaration of Human Rights, www.un.org/en/documents/udhr/, accessed April 2013.
7   The International Convention on Economic, Social and Cultural Rights, http://www.ohchr.org/EN/ProfessionalInterest/Pages/CESCR.aspx, accessed April 2013. .
8   Martin Luther King Jr., "Where Do We Go From Here?" Annual Report delivered at the 11th Convention of the Southern Christian Leadership Conference, Atlanta, GA, August 16, 1967.
9   Corbett B. Daly, "Home Foreclosures in 2010 Top One Million For the First Time," Reuters, January 13, 2011. www.reuters.com/article/2011/01/13/us-usa-housing-foreclosures-idUSTRE70C0YD20110113
    There is no data about how many people or families lived in these one million houses. However, because many of these foreclosed houses were multifamily houses, including large apartment buildings, it is likely that more than 3,000 families were displaced each day.
10 Anna Julia Cooper, "The Early Years in Washington: Reminiscences of Life with the Grimkés" (1951). Quoted in *The Voice of Anna Julia Cooper*, eds. Charles Lemert and Esme Bhan (Oxford: Rowman & Littlefield Publishing, 1998), p. 4.
11 Lorraine Hansberry, *A Raisin in the Sun* (New York: Random House Inc., 1995), pp. 76–77.
12 Gwendolyn Brooks, *A Street in Bronzeville* (New York: Harper and Brothers, 1945).
13 *Webster's Revised Unabridged Dictionary*, 1913 Edition. Available online at: http://machaut.uchicago.edu/?resource=Webster%27s&word=home&use1913=on
14 John Hollander, "It All Depends," *Social Research: An International Quarterly*. Vol. 58, No. 1 (Spring 1991), pp. 31–49.
15 Paula Chakravartty and Denise Ferreira da Silva, "Accumulation, Dispossession, and Debt: The Racial Logic of Global Capitalism," *American Quarterly*, Vol. 64, No. 3 (September 2012), p. 362.
16 Anita Hill, *Reimagining Equality: Stories of Gender, Race, and Finding Home* (Boston: Beacon Press, 2011), p. 116.
17 Joseph W. Singer, "Democratic Estates: Property Law in a Free and Democratic Society," *Cornell Law Review*. Vol. 94. (2009). Available online at: www.lawschool.cornell.edu/research/cornell-law-review/upload/94-4-Singer-Essay.pdf
18 John Locke, *The Second Treatise on Civil Government: Great Books in Philosophy Series* (Amherst: Prometheus Books, 1986), p. 20.

19   G.W.F. Hegel, *Elements of the Philosophy of Right*, trans. T.M. Knox (1821). Quoted in Margaret Jane Radin, "Property and Personhood," *Stanford Law Review*, Vol. 34, No. 5 (May, 1982), p. 973.

20   Margalynne J. Armstrong, "African Americans and Property Ownership: Creating Our Own Meanings, Redefining Our Relationships," *Santa Clara Law Digital Commons*, Vol. 1, No. 1 (1994), p. 81-82. Available at: http://digitalcommons.law.scu.edu/cgi/viewcontent.cgi?article=1308&context=facpubs. Note: italics are my addition.

21   No government agency nor private company has undertaken the task of quantitatively documenting the number of *people* who have been evicted and displaced. However, the most widely accepted estimate is around 10 million people. The methodology is as follows: Since the crisis began in late 2007, bankers have executed foreclosures on approximately four million homes, according to data from both Core Logic and Realty Trac, two of the leading industry data providers. [www.realtytrac.com/content/news-and-opinion/foreclosure-settlement-helps-lift-foreclosure-millstone-dragging-down-housing-market-7019; http://agbeat.com/real-estate-news-events/nearly-four-million-foreclosures-completed-since-housing-crash-began/]
      The Center for Responsible Lending estimates that more than 80 percent of those homes were occupied [www.responsiblelending.org/mortgage-lending/research-analysis/lost-ground-2011.html]. The National Low Income Housing Coalition has shown that 20 percent were multifamily apartment buildings. [http://nlihc.org/library/other/periodic/rif2012]. As of the 2010 Census, there were 113 million occupied households, with an average household size of 2.6 people. On average, then, the 4 million house foreclosures would affect about 11.5 million people. Due to various other factors (some specific states, for example, protect renters in foreclosed properties from eviction), I and others round the number down to a conservative estimate of 10 million.

22   As of the 2010 Census, Michigan had the eighth-highest population of all the United States, with 8,883,360 residents.
      U.S. Census. U.S. Census Bureau: State and County QuickFacts: Michigan (Bureau of the Census), 2010. Available at http://quickfacts.census.gov/qfd/states/26000.html

23   "The Financial Crisis Report in Charts" *The Department of the Treasury.* April 2012. Available at: www.treasury.gov/resource-center/data-chart-center/Documents/20120413_FinancialCrisisResponse.pdf
      Note: It is important to remember that this number reflects pre-crash speculative home equity values; their dizzying rise helped trigger the crisis itself.

24   Mc Nelly Torres, "Poverty, Homelessness, Rising Sharply Among Florida Students," *Florida Center for Investigative Reporting* (in Partnership with NPR) February 14, 2012. http://stateimpact.npr.org/florida/2012/02/14/poverty-homelessness-rising-sharply-among-florida-students/

25   Debbie Gruenstein Bocian, Wei Li, Carolina Reid, *Lost Ground, 2011: Disparities in Mortgage Lending and Foreclosures,*,Center for Responsible Lending (Chapel Hill: University of North Carolina, November 2011), p. 4.

26   Throughout the course of my travels, I also interviewed many Hispanic families. The Hispanic families who were facing foreclosure or other types of housing instability often related the experience of displacement to immigration issues and U.S. imperialism abroad. They also explained that navigating the U.S. housing system was particularly difficult because of language barriers. Some expressed frustrations with U.S. economic and military interventions in Latin America, which drove millions north to the United States each year, only to experience not only immigration difficulties but also high rates of foreclosure and eviction. This narrative is an important and unique story that I hope someone will write. However, I chose to focus

specifically on the African American community in the U.S. in order to best illuminate the history and complexities of this particular struggle, rather than group all people of color into a story that would be defined, ultimately, by their otherness.

27   Bocian et al., *Lost Ground, 2011*, p. 15.

28   Jessica Silver-Greenberg, "Bank Deal Ends Flawed Reviews of Foreclosures," *New York Times*, January 10, 2013. www.nytimes.com/2013/01/11/business/bank-deal-ends-flawed-reviews-of-foreclosures.html

29   Bocian et al., *Lost Ground, 2011*, p. 18. Note: The data set included only mortgages that were either originated or refinanced between 2004 and 2008.

30   *Ibid.*, p. 19.

31   Among African Americans, low-income borrowers had an 11 percent rate of eviction; moderate-income borrowers a 10 percent rate of eviction; middle-income borrowers a 9.5 percent rate of eviction, and higher-income borrowers a 9.9 percent rate of eviction. *Ibid.*, p. 20.

32   *Ibid.*, p. 21.

33   Hill, *Reimagining Equality*, p. xv.

34   In fact, a few Blacks owned land even under the institution of slavery, as Dylan Penningroth uncovers in *The Claims of Kinfolk: African American Property and Community in the Nineteenth-Century South* (Chapel Hill: University of North Carolina Press, 2003). However, the early Reconstruction era was a turning point in the possibility for mass landownership for the former slaves.

35   These men and women were called "the freedmen" because the Fourteenth Amendment, which granted African Americans full citizenship, had not yet been passed.

36   W.E.B. Dubois, *The Souls of Black Folk* in *Three Negro Classics* (New York: Avon Books, 1965), p. 228.

37   *Ibid.*, p. 214.

38   Toni Morrison and Robert Stepto, "Intimate Things in Place: A Conversation with Toni Morrison," *Massachusetts Review*, Vol. 18, No. 3 (Autumn 1977), p. 486.

39   August Wilson, *Fences* (New York: Samuel French, Inc., 1986), p. 50.

40   Ralph Ellison, *Invisible Man* (New York: Random House, 1952).

41   Stokely Carmichael, "What We Want," *New York Review of Books*, Vol. 7 (September 22, 1966), pp. 5-6, 8. Available at www.nybooks.com/articles/archives/1966/sep/22/what-we-want/?pagination=false

42   George W. Bush, speech at the White House Conference on Minority Homeownership. October 15, 2002. Speech text available online at the Public Papers of the Presidents of the United States from the U.S. Government Printing Office. www.gpo.gov/fdsys/pkg/PPP-2002-book2/html/PPP-2002-book2-doc-pg1807.htm

43   Jim Cullen, *The American Dream: The Short History of an Idea that Shaped a Nation* (Oxford: Oxford University Press, 2003), p. 139.

44   United States Census Bureau, *2010 Census of Population and Housing: Lee County, North Carolina* (Washington, DC: US Bureau of the Census), www.census.gov/popfinder/?fl=37105
     United States Census Bureau, *Population of Counties by Decennial Census: 1900 to 1990, Lee County, North Carolina* (Washington DC, US Bureau of the Census). www.census.gov/population/cencounts/nc190090.txt

45   For more information, see: Dolores Hayden, *Building Suburbia* (New York: Random House, 2003).

46   US Census Bureau, *Historical Census of Housing Tables: Homeownership Rates* (Washington D.C., US Bureau of the Census). www.census.gov/housing/census/data/owner/owner_tab.txt

US Census Bureau News, *Residential Vacancies and Homeownership Rates in the Third Quarter of 2012* (Washington, DC, US Bureau of the Census, Social, Economic, and Housing Statistics Division, October 30, 2012), Table 4: Homeownership Rates for the United States 1995 to 2012. www.census.gov/housing/hvs/files/qtr312/q312press.pdf

47   Isabel Wilkerson, *The Warmth of Other Suns* (New York: Random House, 2010), p. 11.

48   Ibid.

49   FHA lending manual from the 1930s, quoted in Vincent Cannato, "A Home of One's Own," *National Affairs*, Issue 3, Spring 2010. www.nationalaffairs.com/publications/detail/a-home-of-ones-own

50   Thomas D. Sugrue, *The Origins of the Urban Crisis: Race and Inequality in PostWar Detroit* (Princeton: Princeton University Press, 1996), pp. 63-72. Quoted in Dolores Hayden, *Building Suburbia* (New York: Random House, 2003), pp. 111–112.

51   US Census Bureau, *State and County Quick Facts: Levittown, New York*. Population, 2010: 51,881 http://quickfacts.census.gov/qfd/states/36/3642081.html

52   Federal Housing Administration, *FHA Loan Requirements*. www.fha.com/fha_loan_requirements.cfm

53   Quotes from video by Bob Ingalls: www.youtube.com/watch?v=Y8dfiVzL11U

54   Ibid.

55   Kelli Gauthier, "Chasing a Dream," *Chattanooga Times Free Press*, May 29, 2011. www.timesfreepress.com/news/2011/may/29/chasing-dream/

56   Walt Whitman, "Wicked Architecture," in Life Illustrated, 1856. Reprinted in Emory Holloway, ed., Walt Whitman, Complete Poetry and Selected Prose and Letters (London: The Nonesuch Press, 1938), 607.

57   Isabel Wilkerson, *The Warmth of Other Suns* (New York: Random House, 2010), p. 12.

58   "Chicago Closes Cabrini-Green Project," Associated Press, 2010. www.usatoday.com/news/nation/2010-12-01-cabrini-green_N.htm

59   Angela Caputo, "Forgotten People," *The Chicago Reporter*, September 24, 2007. www.chicagoreporter.com/news/2007/09/forgotten-people

60   David Harvey, "The Crises of Capitalism" Renaissance Society of America speech, April 26, 2010. http://dotsub.com/view/a241d747-ffa4-4593-bba7-a04bb4323358/viewTranscript/eng

61   Herb Weisbaum, "Debt Collectors Getting More Aggressive," MSNBC, August 14, 2008. www.msnbc.msn.com/id/26178152/ns/business-consumer_news/t/debt-collectors-getting-more-aggressive/

62   *Dillon v. Select Portfolio Servicing*, Case No. 09-1469. (C.A. 1, Jan. 13, 2011). http://judicialview.com/Court-Cases/Civil-Procedure/Dillon-v-Select-Portfolio-Servicing/10/21599

63   Rich Phillips, "Woman Sues Debt Collector over Husband's Death," *CNN*, December 10, 2009. http://articles.cnn.com/2009-12-10/living/debt.collector.lawsuit_1_debt-collectors-green-tree-servicing-credit-and-collection-professionals?_s=PM:LIVING

64   IMC Mortgage Company dissolved in 2001. There is no longer any contact information for the company and there exists no record that Griggs did not pay his September 1998 payment.

65   *Inside Job*, written by Charles Ferguson (Sony Pictures, 2010). Transcript: http://moviecultists.com/wp-content/uploads/screenplays/inside-job.pdf

66   See the 2002 FTC Complaint and Settlement with Mercantile Mortgage Company. www.ftc.gov/os/caselist/0023321.shtm

67   See www.ftc.gov/opa/2002/07/subprimelendingcases.shtm for a list of subprime lending fraud settlements. The last example, the company that the FTC accused of foreclosing on families who had not defaulted on their payments, was Capital City Mortgage Corporation.

68   Yves Smith, "Bank of America foreclosure reviews: whistleblowers reveal extensive borrower harm and orchestrated coverup (part II)" *Naked Capitalism,* January 22, 2013. www.nakedcapitalism.com/2013/01/37705.html

69   "Fairbanks Capital Settles FTC and HUD Charges," FTC Press Release, November 12, 2003. www.ftc.gov/opa/2003/11/fairbanks.shtm

70   Dakin Campbell and Lorraine Woellert, "Ally Says GMAC Mortgage Mishandled Affidavits on Foreclosures," Bloomberg News, September 21, 2010. www.bloomberg.com/news/2010-09-21/ally-financial-says-gmac-mortgage-mishandled-affidavits-on-foreclosures.html

71   Campbell and Woellert, "Ally Says GMAC Mortgage Mishandled Affidavits on Foreclosures, Bloomberg News, September 21, 2010. *Ibid.*

72   Zach Carter "Deutsche Bank Sues Foreclosure Fraud Expert's Son with No Financial Interest in Her Case" *Huffington Post,* May 13, 2007. www.huffingtonpost.com/2011/05/13/deutsche-bank-lynn-szymoniak_n_861900.html. See embedded video of *60 Minutes* interview.

73   Nelson D. Schwartz and J.B. Silver-Greenberg, "Bank Officials Cited in Churn of Foreclosures," *New York Times,* March 12, 2012. www.nytimes.com/2012/03/13/business/federal-report-cites-bank-officials-in-foreclosure-surge.html?pagewanted=all

       As a result of the robo-signing scandal, the five largest banks settled with the federal government, paying $25 billion that was supposed to go directly to mortgage-holding families. Some of the money, instead, has gone to paying off state deficits, budget shortfalls that were caused by the banks themselves.

74   For more on the SEC: www.sec.gov/about/whatwedo.shtml

75   Some cycled back and forth between Wall Street and K Street as fast as their private planes could take them. Roger Altman, for example, started as a partner at the later-to-collapse Lehman Brothers, served a stint as assistant secretary of the treasury, turned to Wall Street to work in investment banking at Lehman and as the head of mergers and acquisitions at Blackstone, served as deputy treasury secretary under Clinton, returned to Blackstone, and finally became an advisor for both Kerry in 2004 and Clinton in 2008.

76   *Wimbley v. Select Portfolio Servicing.* In the U.S. District Court for the Middle District of North Carolina, July 9, 2009. http://nc.findacase.com/research/wfrmDocViewer.aspx/xq/fac.20090709_0000120.MNC.htm/qx

77   Joe Nocera, "The Foreclosure Fiasco," *New York Times,* January 14, 2013.

78   Elvin Wyly, C.S. Ponder, Pierson Nettling, Bosco Ho, Sophie Ellen Fung, Zachary Liebowitz, and Dan Hammel, "New Racialized Meanings of Housing in America," *American Quarterly,* Vol. 64, No. 3, September 2012, p. 575.

79   Debbie Gruenstein Bocian, Wei Li, and Carolina Reid, *Lost Ground, 2011: Disparities in Mortgage Lending and Foreclosures,* Center for Responsible Lending (Chapel Hill: University of North Carolina, November 2011), p. 8.

80   Ofelia O. Cuervas, "Welcome to My Cell: Housing and Race in the Mirror of American Democracy," *American Quarterly* Vol. 64, No. 3, September 2012, p. 613.

81   Testimonies in: John P. Relman et al., "Plaintiff Mayor and City Council of Baltimore's Memorandum of Points and Authorities in Opposition to Defendants' Motion to Dismiss the Amended Complaint," *Mayor and City Council of Baltimore vs. Wells Fargo.* Document 133, filed 10/16/09. Available online at: www.clearinghouse.net/chDocs/public/FH-MD-0001-0009.pdf

82   For more information see the U.S. Department of Justice's complaint against Countrywide, which was the largest lending discrimination lawsuit in DOJ history, leading to a $335 million settlement. The DOJ alleged that Countrywide discriminated against 200,000 families. www.justice.gov/crt/about/hce/documents/countrywidecomp.pdf

83 Testimonies in: John P. Relman, et. al. "Plaintiff Mayor and City Council of Baltimore's Memorandum of Points and Authorities in Opposition to Defendants' Motion to Dismiss the Amended Complaint," *Mayor and City Council of Baltimore vs. Wells Fargo.* Document 133, filed 10/16/09. Available online at: www.clearinghouse.net/chDocs/public/FH-MD-0001-0009. pdf

84 Benjamin Howell, "Exploiting Race and Space: Concentrated Subprime Lending as Housing Discrimination," *California Law Review,* Vol. 94, Issue 1, January 2006. http://scholarship.law. berkeley.edu/californialawreview/vol94/iss1/3

85 Dan Childs, "Foreclosure-Related Suicide: a Sign of the Times?" *ABC News,* July 25, 2008. http://abcnews.go.com/Health/DepressionNews/story?id=5444573&page=1

86 "Foreclosure Threat Drives Some to Suicide," *CBS News,* March 24, 2012. www.cbsnews.com/ stories/2010/03/24/national/main6329383.shtml

87 "Ohio Woman, 90, Attempts Suicide After Foreclosure," *Reuters,* October 3, 2008. http://www. reuters.com/article/2008/10/03/us-foreclosure-shooting-idUSTRE4928IS20081003

88 Alan Macher, "Ocala," in *Where to Retire,* May/June 2012, pp. 62-68.

89 Meghan Neal and Erik Ortiz, "Man kills himself days before eviction from California home in foreclosure," *New York Daily News,* May 23, 2012. www.nydailynews.com/news/national/man-kills-days-eviction-california-home-foreclosure-article-1.1083046

   "Three dead in New Years Day foreclosure murder suicide," *CUCollector.com.* http://blog. cucollector.com/hot-topics/three-dead-in-foreclosure-murder-suicide/

   "Georgia police say man known as 'chicken man' is presumed dead in home explosion," *Fox News,* March 27, 2012. www.foxnews.com/us/2012/03/27/georgia-police-say-man-known-as-chicken-man-may-have-blown-up-home-to-avoid/

   Evan Bedard, "Houston couple commits suicide after being faced with foreclosure," *LoanSafe.org,* May 17, 2010. www.loansafe.org/houston-couple-commits-suicide-after-being-faced-with-foreclosure

90 The Greenspan's Body Count project. http://greenspansbodycount.blogspot.com/

91 Nick Turse, "The Body Count on Main Street," *In These Times,* December 19, 2008.http:// inthesetimes.com/article/4101/the_body_count_on_main_street/

92 Jerry Goldberg, "How the Banks Destroyed Detroit," *Workers World,* March 31, 2011. www. workers.org/2011/us/banks_destroyed_detroit_0407/

93 Foreclosure data from personal interviews with Steve Babson, a professor at Wayne State University in Detroit, who analyzed foreclosure data from RealtyTrac.

94 Goldberg, "How the Banks Destroyed Detroit."

95 International Monetary Fund, *World Economic Outlook: Growth Resuming, Dangers Remain,* Chapter 3: Dealing with Household Debt, April 2012, p. 99. www.imf.org/external/pubs/ft/ weo/2012/01/pdf/c3.pdf

96 "Home Wreckers: How Wall Street Foreclosures Are Devastating our Communities." http:// dig.abclocal.go.com/kgo/PDF/Home-Wreckers-Report.pdf

97 Ibid.

98 The figures represent 110,000 bank foreclosures multiplied by $2,000 and $19,000, respectively.

99 Bill Vlasic and Steven Yaccino, "Detroit Waits, Apprehensive, for Manager to Take Over," the *New York Times,* March 23, 2013. www.nytimes.com/2013/03/24/us/defiant-anxious-detroit-gets-an-emergency-manager.html

100 Krissah Thompson, "Possibility of emergency manager in Detroit prompts civil rights concerns," the *Washington Post,* January 5, 2012. http://articles.washingtonpost.com/2012-01-05/ politics/35440087_1_emergency-manager-civil-rights-bettie-buss

101 "Signs Warn of Crackhead Infestation at Detroit Park" *CBS Detroit*, May 17, 2012. http://detroit.cbslocal.com/2012/05/17/signs-warn-of-crackhead-infestation-at-detroit-park/

102 Langston Hughes, "Let America Be America Again," *The Collected Poems of Langston Hughes*, (New York: Alfred A. Knopf, 1994).

103 Matthew Dolan, "Detroit Schools' Cuts Plan Approved," *Wall Street Journal*, February 22, 2011. http://online.wsj.com/article/SB10001424052748703610604576158783513445212.html

104 United States Census Bureau, *Selected Economic Characteristics, 2007-2011 American Community Survey, Five-Year Estimates*, Census Tract 16, Hamilton County, TN (Washington D.C., US Census Bureau).

105 Andy Johns, "Great Depression Provides Perspective on Today's Economy," *Chattanooga Times Free Press*, March 2, 2009. www.timesfreepress.com/news/2009/mar/02/chattanooga-great-depression-provides-perspective-/?mobile

106 David C. Wheelock, "Changing the Rules: State Mortgage Foreclosure Moratoria During the Great Depression," Federal Reserve Bank of St. Louis *Review*, November/December 2008, 90(6), p. 570. http://research.stlouisfed.org/publications/review/08/11/Wheelock.pdf

107 Catherine McNicol Stock, *Main Street in Crisis* (Chapel Hill: University of North Carolina Press, 1992), p. 140

108 State Historical Society of North Dakota online exhibit on Governor William Langer. http://history.nd.gov/exhibits/governors/governors17.html

109 Peter Marcuse, "Interpreting Public Housing History," *Journal of Architectural and Planning Research*, August 1995. Vol. 12, No.. 3, pp. 240–258.

110 Gail Radford, *Modern Housing for America: Policy Struggles in the New Deal Era* (University of Chicago Press), p. 49.

111 Catherine Bauer, *Modern Housing* (Boston: Houghton Mifflin, 1934). Quoted in Gail Radford, *Modern Housing for America: Policy Struggles In the New Deal Era* (Chicago: University of Chicago Press), p. 79.

112 Kenneth T. Jackson, *Crabgrass Frontier: The Suburbanization of the United States* (New York: Oxford University Press, 1985), p. 224

113 Franklin D. Roosevelt, "State of the Union Message to Congress," January 11, 1944. See the American Presidency Project, UC Santa Barbara. www.presidency.ucsb.edu/ws/index.php?pid=16518

114 Alex Kotlowitz, *There Are No Children Here* (New York: Random House, 1991), p. 22.

115 Aaron Cook, "Our Story: Harriet Tubman," 2009. http://hope4theinnercity.org/page/our-story/harriet-tubman

116 William J. Collins and Robert A. Margo, "Race and Homeownership: A Century-Long View," Working Paper for the Department of Economics at Vanderbilt University, May 2000. See Figures 1 and 2. www.vanderbilt.edu/econ/wparchive/workpaper/vu00-w12.pdf

117 J.S. Fuerst, *When Public Housing Was Paradise* (Chicago: University of Illinois Press, 2005), p. 11.

118 Catherine R Squires, "Coloring in the Bubble: Perspectives from Black-Oriented Media on the (Latest) Economic Disaster," *American Quarterly* Vol. 64, No. 3, September 2012, p. 548.

119 "We Call These Projects Home," A Right to the City Alliance Report on Public Housing, May 2010. www.righttothecity.org/index.php/resources/reports/item/61-we-call-these-projects-home

120 United States Census Bureau, *Historical Census of Housing Tables: Homeownership Rates* (Washington, DC, US Bureau of the Census). www.census.gov/housing/census/data/owner/owner_tab.txt

121 Collins and Margo, "Race and Homeownership," Table 4. www.vanderbilt.edu/econ/wparchive/workpaper/vu00-w12.pdf

122 Elvin Wyly, C.S. Ponder, Pierson Nettling, Bosco Ho, Sophie Ellen Fung, Zachary Liebowitz, and Dan Hammel, "New Racialized Meanings of Housing in America," *American Quarterly*, Vol. 64, No. 3, September 2012, p. 575.

123 Kotlowitz, *There Are No Children Here*, p. 240.

124 Guy Guliotta, "Saving HUD: One Department's Risky Strategy for Radical Change," *Washington Post*, February 6, 1995. www.highbeam.com/doc/1P2-819765.html

125 "We Call These Projects Home," A Right to the City Alliance Report on Public Housing, May 2010, p. 45.

126 Ibid., p. 13.

127 Yolanda Putman, "Chattanooga Switching to More Vouchers, Less Public Housing," *Chattanooga Times Free Press*, May 31, 2011. www.timesfreepress.com/news/2011/may/31/chattanooga-switching-more-vouchers-less-public-ho/

128 Mike Pare, "Chattanooga Ranks Third in Apartment Cost Growth," *Chattanooga Times Free Press*, January 19, 2012. www.timesfreepress.com/news/2012/jan/19/city-ranks-no-3-in-apartment-cost-growth/?businesstnvalley

129 National Alliance to End Homelessness, "State of Homelessness in 2012," Chapter One: Homeless Counts, January 17, 2012. www.endhomelessness.org/library/entry/soh-2012-chapter-one-homelessness-counts

130 Talmadge Wright, *Out of Place: Homeless Mobilizations, Subcities, and Contested Landscapes* (Albany: State University of New York Press, 1997), p. 21.

131 National Alliance to End Homelessness, "State of Homelessness in 2012," Chapter One: Homeless Counts, January 17, 2012. www.endhomelessness.org/library/entry/soh-2012-chapter-one-homelessness-counts

132 U.S. soldier death count: http://icasualties.org. Chicago murder rate from annual Chicago Murder Analysis report https://portal.chicagopolice.org/portal/page/portal/ClearPath/News/Statistical percent20Reports/Murder percent20Reports/MA11.pdf

133 Melisa Chadburn, "Banks Booting Families and Leaving Homes to Rot," *AlterNet*, June 11, 2012. www.alternet.org/story/155734/banks_booting_families_and_leaving_homes_to_rot percent3A_a_tour_of_blighted_homes_in_los_angeles?paging=off

134 Norimitsu Onishi, "Foreclosed Houses Become Homes for Indoor Marijuana Farms," *New York Times*, May 6, 2012. www.nytimes.com/2012/05/07/us/marijuana-growers-move-to-the-suburbs.html

135 Chris Barton, "Occupy Auckland Protest Speaks with Many Voices," *New Zealand Herald*, October 29, 2011. www.nzherald.co.nz/nz/news/article.cfm?c_id=1&objectid=10762353

136 www.occupyraleigh.org/2012/04/defend-homes-from-invading-banks-data-and-direct-action-on-the-foreclosure-crisis/

137 "Man Killed in Icy Detroit Crash." *CBS Detroit*. January 30, 2012. http://detroit.cbslocal.com/2012/01/30/man-killed-in-icy-detroit-crash/

138 Quotes from video by Bob Ingalls: www.youtube.com/watch?v=Y8dfiVzL11U

139 Halah Touryalai, "Detroit Pension Funds Hit BNY Mellon with $1 Billion Class Action Suit," *Forbes*, September 13, 2011. www.forbes.com/sites/halahtouryalai/2011/09/13/detroit-pension-funds-hit-bny-mellon-with-1-billion-class-action-suit

140 Ben Rooney, "Bank of New York Named in Currency Fraud Suit," *CNN Money*, October 5. 2011. http://money.cnn.com/2011/10/05/news/companies/bank_new_york_mellon_fraud/

141 Ed Denson, "Pepper Spray, Pain and Justice," *Civil Liberties*, Winter 1998. www.civilliberties.org/win98spray.html

142   Eric Roper and Nicole Norfleet, "Foreclosure Protest Puts Minneapolis Officials in Tight Spot," [Minneapolis] *Star Tribune,* May 31, 2012. www.startribune.com/local/minneapolis/156108395.html?page=1&c=y&refer=y

143   Christopher Matthews, "Why Is Ed DeMarco Blocking a Win-Win Housing Program?" *Time,* August 1, 2012. http://business.time.com/2012/08/01/why-is-ed-demarco-blocking-a-win-win-housing-program/

144   J.D. Heyes, "Iceland Forgives Mortgage Debt to Save Its Economy," *Natural News,* May 6, 2012. www.naturalnews.com/035779_Iceland_mortgage_debt_economy.html

145   Al Goodman, "Spanish banks stop evictions for the next two years in cases of 'extreme necessity' " *CNN,* November 12, 2012. http://edition.cnn.com/2012/11/12/business/spain-home-evictions/index.html

146   Quotes from video by Bob Ingalls: www.youtube.com/watch?v=Y8dfiVzL11U

147   Yolanda Putman, "Chattanooga Housing Authority to Meet Today with Residents and Mayor Ron Littlefield," *Chattanooga Times Free Press,* April 9, 2012. www.timesfreepress.com/news/2012/apr/09/chattanooga-housing-authority-meeting-today-public/

148   "Our Purpose," Purpose Built website. http://purposebuiltcommunities.org/our-purpose/our-purpose.html

149   Yolanda Putman, "Atlanta Based Nonprofit Purpose Built Community May Come to Chattanooga," *Chattanooga Times Free Press,* December 12, 2011. www.timesfreepress.com/news/2011/dec/12/atlanta-based-nonprofit-may-come-chattanooga/

150   Jacqueline Trescott, "Music of the Movement," *Washington Post,* August 19, 2011. www.washingtonpost.com/blogs/arts-post/post/music-of-the-movement-aint-gonna-let-nobody-turn-me-round/2011/08/18/gIQA5GxkNJ_blog.html

151   Don Terry, "Foreclosed Home Is a Risky Move for Homeless Family," *New York Times,* June 25, 2011. www.nytimes.com/2011/06/26/us/26cnchomeless.html?_r=0

152   Jason Lange, "Home resales fall, housing recovery still on track," *Reuters,* January 22, 2013. www.reuters.com/article/2013/01/22/us-usa-economy-idUSBRE90E0KL20130122

153   Ibid. and Chris Isidore, "Economists: housing recovery finally here," *CNN Money,* October 3, 2012. http://money.cnn.com/2012/10/02/news/economy/housing-recovery-economists/index.html

154   Emmanuel Saez, "Striking It Richer: The Evolution of Top Incomes in the United States," March 2, 2012. Available at: http://elsa.berkeley.edu/~saez/saez-UStopincomes-2010.pdf

155   Ylan Q. Mui, "For black Americans, financial damage from subprime implosion is likely to last," *Washington Post,* July 8, 2012. http://articles.washingtonpost.com/2012-07-08/business/35486457_1_credit-scores-auto-loan-financial-crisis

156   Anita Hill, *Reimagining Equality: Stories of Gender, Race, and Finding Home* (Boston: Beacon Press, 2011), p. 116.

157   Peter Eavis, "In Tighter Loan Rules, Wiggle Room for Banks," *New York Times,* January 10, 2013. http://dealbook.nytimes.com/2013/01/10/in-tighter-loan-rules-wiggle-room-for-banks/

158   Edward Wyatt, "U.S. Consumer Watchdog to Issue Mortgage Rules," *New York Times,* January 10, 2013. www.nytimes.com/2013/01/10/business/consumers-win-some-mortgage-safety-in-new-rules.html

159   "Foreclosure Moratorium Support Fades," *UPI,* October 15, 2010. www.upi.com/Top_News/US/2010/10/15/Poll-Foreclosure-moratorium-support-fades/UPI-22751287175120/

160   Chester Hartman, "The Case for a Right to Housing," in *Housing Policy Debate,* Vol. 9, Issue 2 (1998), p. 223. http://faculty.design.umn.edu/jrcrump/pdf/hartman.pdf

After losing her son in Iraq, one East New York mother faced the loss of her home. On December 6, 2011, this mother in mourning joined Occupy Our Homes to speak out against foreclosure. Photo and caption by Michael Alexander Gould-Wartofsky.

INDEX

Photo by Jed Brandt

LAURA GOTTESDIENER is a freelance journalist in New York City. She has written for *The Huffington Post*, the *Arizona Republic*, the *New Haven Advocate*, AlterNet, and *Waging Nonviolence* (wagingnonviolence.org), where she is an associate editor. She won the John Hersey Prize at Yale University for a body of journalistic work and was a national finalist for the Norman Mailer Nonfiction Award for her 2009 investigation of girls' wrestling. She was actively involved in the Occupy movement and lived in Zuccotti Park from early October 2011 until the police raid in mid-November 2011. *A Dream Foreclosed* is her first book.